MAT, MOUNT, AND FRAME IT YOURSELF ·

MAT, MOUNT, AND FRAME IT YOURSELF ·

M. DAVID LOGAN

WATSON-GUPTILL PUBLICATIONS / NEW YORK

Front cover
M. DAVID LOGAN
Memories of the Orient

Frontispiece
JEANNE CARBONETTI
Magic Mountain

Title page
ELAINE STIMEL
Art framed with Nielsen molding and Bainbridge
Artcare matboard.
Photo compliments of NielsenBainbridge.

Acquisitions Editor: Joy Aquilino
Edited by Robbie Capp
Designed by Patricia Fabricant
Graphic production by Ellen Greene
Text set in Adobe Garamond and TheSans

Copyright © 2002 by M. David Logan

First published in 2002 by Watson-Guptill Publications,
a division of VNU Business Media, Inc.
770 Broadway, New York, NY 10003
www.watsonguptill.com

Library of Congress Control Number: 2001093246
ISBN: 0-8230-3038-5

Manufactured in Singapore

First printing, 2002

2 3 4 5 6 7 8 / 09 08 07 06 05 04 03 02

FOR CAMBELLE,
WHOSE GOOD-HEARTED SPIRIT
HAS FRAMED THIS WORK

ACKNOWLEDGMENTS

This book could not have been produced without the help of several people, principally Joy Aquilino, Robbie Capp, Patricia Fabricant, John Zachrel, and Leonard May. I would like to extend a special thanks to my photographer, Sarah Bacci, whose skills and tenacity made this vision a reality, and to my dear Sally Alatalo, whose talent and ingenuity at the eleventh hour brought the ship safely into port.

ABOUT THE AUTHOR

For over fifteen years, M. David Logan has taught matting and framing as a member of the faculty at The School of the Art Institute of Chicago, at Harper College, and in his own workshops and seminars held throughout the United States. As a contributing editor for *The Artists' Magazine* and as the editor and publisher of the monthly newsletter *The Self Framer's Advisor,* he has written numerous articles on the subject, and is featured in the video "Mat Cutting Made Easy." Based in Palatine, Illinois, the author owns a business dedicated to providing know-how to those who want to do their own picture framing.

TABLE OF CONTENTS

INTRODUCTION   9
    Beginners to Pros   10

Step 1: DETERMINING MEASUREMENTS & PROPORTIONS 13
    Planning ahead   14
    Rules to Live By   18
    Looking Good, Saving Money and Time   21

Step 2: SELECTING COLORS FOR MATS & FRAMES   31
    Color Balance   32
    Frames and Accents   36

Step 3: CHOOSING MATERIALS & EQUIPMENT   39
    Materials: Matboard   40
    Foamboard   43
    Glazing Materials   44
    Frames   46
    Mounting Materials   51
    Hardware   55
    Other Essential Materials   57
    Essential Permanent Equipment   59
    Further Option: Equipment for Making Frames   65

Step 4: PREPARING MATERIALS   69
    Sizing Matboard Like a Pro   70
    How to Size Glazing   74
    Making Frames from Scratch   75
    Sanding and Finishing Molding   80
    Preparing an Object Box   81

Step 5: CUTTING MAT WINDOWS   83

    How to Get Good Results Consistently   84
    Basic Single Mat   88
    Double Mat   90
    Multiple-Opening Mat   92
    Double Multiple-Opening Mat   95
    Title Indent Mat   98
    Title Window Mat   100
    Stepped-Corner Mat   103
    Eight-Sided Window Mat   105
    Oval or Round Mat   107
    V-Groove Mat   111

Step 6: MOUNTING   115

    Conservation Framing   116
    Museum Framing   117
    Safe, Regular Framing   118
    Permanent Mounting   120
    Removable Mounting   123
    Elevation Mounting: Pastel Art   128
    Mounting Needlework   129
    Mounting Three-Dimensional Objects   131

Step 7: ASSEMBLING FRAMES   135

    Metal Sectional Frames   136
    Chopped and Routed Wood Frames   137
    Cutting and Joining Length Molding   138

Step 8: GLAZING, INSTALLING, & HANGING FRAMED ART   141

    Glazing   142
    Installing the Artwork Sandwich   144
    Frame Fitting   145
    Attaching Hanging Hardware   152
    Hanging Artwork   154

Afterword   155
Resources   156
Index   158

PETER WEST
Dragon Train 136

Painters who do their own framing not only economize; they also
maintain full artistic control over the presentation of their work.

INTRODUCTION

There was a time, not long ago, when picture framing was the exclusive province of the professional, when equipment and materials for do-it-yourself framing were inferior or unavailable. But those days have passed. Now, anyone who wants to mat, mount, and frame can—and that reality has opened new inroads for aspiring professionals, as well.

In the past, in order to open a frame shop, you had to make a substantial investment in equipment, fixtures, and inventory, sold to you by a wholesaler, who, you would hope, would also be willing to train you. Woe unto you should you find out later that picture framing didn't suit you, or that you were not particularly gifted at it. The industry had few provisions for those who wanted to start slowly, and none at all for those who wanted to frame for themselves, without going into business.

These days, more and more picture framers are entering the ranks of the pros through the backdoor. More and more are starting out as do-it-yourself framers and reaching such a level of competence and business savvy servicing friends and neighbors that they end up as professionals. Truly, this is a good thing because it lets people ease into picture framing at their own speed and allows them to take the craft as far as they comfortably are able, without risk of debt. It's worth noting that at-home framing is increasingly attractive to retirees, many of whom prefer to pursue a business objective at their own pace—and then withdraw if they so choose. Since it offers such options, do-it-yourself framing is ideal. It's a rewarding hobby that contains the potential to be something more, but only if you want it to be.

BEGINNERS TO PROS

This book is written for a wide range of readers. For beginner and hobbyist framers, the text assumes no previous knowledge on the part of the reader, and as it proceeds in methodical fashion, each step builds a foundation of knowledge that informs later sections. These pages are also for knowledge-hungry professionals, as they provide a broad understanding of the step-by-step process, give insights into a wide range of materials and techniques, and delve deeply into common problems and practical ways to solve them.

Artists of all types can also benefit from this book: painters and graphic artists who have long understood the expediency of doing their own framing, not only to economize, but in order to maintain artistic control over the presentation of their work; photographers who know the importance of careful oversight at every step in a project; and woodworkers who approach picture framing from their own skilled perspective. Finally, for other crafters and collectors who have no more interest in operating a miter saw than they do in changing an oil filter, this book's simplified methods will be especially welcome.

KEYS TO ECONOMIZING

There is room for everyone in the world of picture framing; it is a delightfully flexible enterprise that can be carried out on your kitchen table in the time it takes to whip up a soufflé. In fact, you can have picture framing any way you want it, but you'll have to make the right choices, the ones that will present the work you frame in the way you envision it, the way you will find most gratifying. The pages ahead will show you how to make the right choices, guiding you through the procedures needed to mat, mount, and frame—and how to do it inexpensively. Of course, you may opt to spend more money, but if you do, it will be based on informed choices made with the understanding of what you are buying, as well as what you are giving up if you decide to spend less.

You will find that good framing, guided by your personal taste and objectives, is a very satisfying craft. Even if you undertake projects that are expensive and elaborate, they would be still more costly if you were to have them done by a frame shop. In fact, ironically, if racking up savings is your goal, the more ambitious you are, the more savings you stand to enjoy. That's because many framing embellishments cost little or nothing in the way of materials, but cost dearly for professional labor charges in putting it all together. At the other end of the spectrum, working with precut, preassembled, and other ready-made frames will offer you ways to save time and money and still produce handsome, do-it-yourself results —all of which we will explore fully.

On average, doing your own framing puts back into your pocket about 50 percent of the cost of having something framed at a frame shop, so a $100-job in a shop costs about $50 if you do it yourself. With those generous savings, you can look forward to putting lots of money back into your pocket in a short period of time, after you've absorbed the cost of your equipment. Of course, if your equipment costs thousands of dollars, you start from a deep hole. Accordingly, another purpose of this book is to show you how to frame pictures without spending a lot for equipment; you can buy everything you need for less than $350. When you look at the broader picture, that money is well spent. By saving $50 each time you frame, you need frame only seven times to absorb the cost of your initital $350 investment. After that, it's money in your pocket. Do you have seven frame jobs in you? If you do, you are ready to start framing.

HAROLD SUDMAN
Orchid
The choice of mat and frame colors, carefully coordinated
to the art, produces a well-unified presentation.

ISSA SHOJAEI

Art framed with Nielsen molding and Bainbridge Artcare matboards.

Photo compliments of NielsenBainbridge.

DETERMINING MEASUREMENTS & PROPORTIONS

Before you begin a framing project, ask yourself several important questions. First, what is your purpose in framing this piece? In other words, where do you envision it ending up? Will it hang in a room in your home, or will it be sold to someone else? Will it be presented proudly as an example of superior artistry, or will it be used to offset a sofa? Will it be scrutinized and evaluated in a juried exhibition, or will it hang unobtrusively in a hallway, waiting for a passerby to notice its qualities? These are important questions that must be answered if you hope to make the right choices in framing any piece.

Another important consideration is what your objectives are in framing it. Do you want to give it a finished, professional look, brought in at a reasonable price, and leave it at that? Or do you want to enhance it in a way that will trumpet your mastery, to heck with the cost. Or perhaps you want to economize; a professional look, yes, but nothing overboard. You need to decide up front how you will budget yourself. The answers to these questions will guide you throughout the project, helping you to make the right choices and bringing you the results you want.

PLANNING AHEAD

Picture framing is more like adding a deck to your home than making dinner from a recipe. Not that it's anywhere as involved as adding a deck, just that it's a project that requires you to make plans before you start. So it would be a mistake to buy materials before you know what you need. That seems obvious, yet, one of the most common mistakes aspiring framers make is not being able to resist the urge to buy cheap frames at garage sales and the like, thinking they'll save money. More often than not, they end up compromising the aesthetics of the piece to effect a clumsy fit, or they end up buying a second frame to make it look right. A more economical approach is to plan carefully before buying anything.

To Mat or Not to Mat

Much of the planning in picture framing involves measuring, but first you must know what has to be measured. So right from the start, decide whether or not you will mat the piece. A mat is the paperboard border surrounding the art. Since the mat is often an essential ingredient in fitting the art to the frame, its measurement is critical. But how do you know whether to add a mat?

Generally, most art on paper is presented with a mat, while most art on canvas is not, and for good reason. The function of the mat is to provide a separation between the art and the glass. Glass lying in direct contact with art is prone to moisture

EDWARD ALDRICH
Broken Silence
Careful measuring is central to good planning and the first step toward successful framing.

condensation, which appears as a blotching or wrinkling on the face of the art and can cause permanent damage. By lifting the glass out of contact with the art, the problem is solved. Thus, we can assume that any art requiring glass must also require a mat. But it is not quite that simple. Not all art requires glass, and of those that do, many may still not be matted.

Art on canvas requires air circulation through the fibers to prevent the development of rot. Since the introduction of glass tends to retard air circulation, art on canvas is often presented without a mat. This is particularly true of oil paintings where the surface can be cleaned directly. For other types of art, where the medium is too sensitive to be touched, glass may be desired to keep away dust and dirt. For example, cross-stitch and other needlework on canvas needs glass, but there should be an adequate space between the work and the glass to promote air circulation. Sometimes the thickness of a mat is not enough. In those cases, spacers are brought into play.

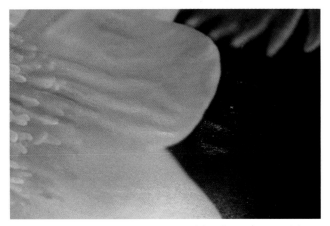

Moisture condensation can cause blotching or wrinkling on the art.

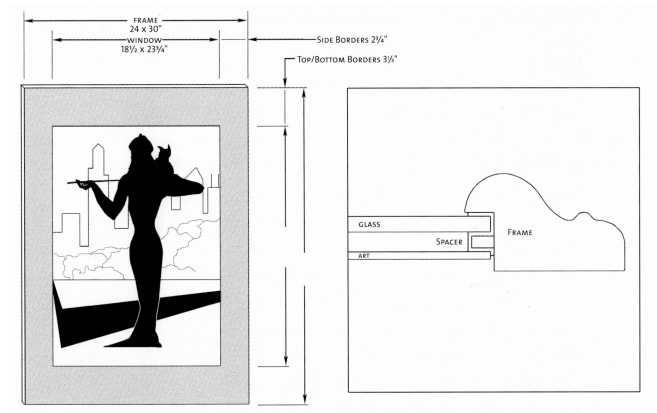

FITTING ART TO FRAME

Using a mat, you can make odd-size art fit into a standard-size frame.

COMMERCIAL SPACERS

When more separation is desired to keep glass farther away from the art, commercial spacers are helpful.

Illustration courtesy of Frametek, Inc.

Spacers

Long, narrow strips of material called spacers can be placed along the edges of artwork and concealed under the lip of the frame to prevent the art from touching the glass. Spacers can be bought or you can make them from strips of foamboard or matboard. Commercial spacers are made of archival-quality plastic and come in a variety of sizes up to ¾", providing adequate air space for the glazing of canvas, if need be. They are also used to separate glass from art when matting seems impractical but glazing is called for, as in the case of very large artwork. Posters are an example. Typically presented under glass, posters are often quite large to begin with and become cumbersome with a mat added. Spacers brought into play allow the glazing of large posters without matting.

Measuring for Matting

Art that is framed sans mat is really quite simple to measure. Since the art is the same size as the frame, all you have to do is measure the size of the art, then buy the glass and frame in the same size. But measuring for art that includes a mat is something else altogether.

Although measuring for matting is more complicated, it rewards you by providing greater flexibility in your choice of frame sizes. If you make your own frames, this is not an issue, since you can make the frame any size you want. But making your own frames may not be your cup of tea—and one of the central purposes of this book is precisely to show how to frame without cutting and constructing frames from scratch. So, assuming you will not construct frames, you should maximize your ability to acquire the best ready-made frames at the best prices with the least hassle. Matting can help you do that.

As an example, let's go back to the frame mentioned above, a poster framed under glass without a mat. For the sake of argument, let's assume that the poster is a reasonable size and not so large that matting it is impractical. Let's also assume that the poster is *not* in a standard size. Standard sizes are those that will fit the greatest number of two-dimensional objects you might buy, objects that are themselves in standard sizes. Preassembled picture frames (and precut lengths of frame that you put together easily) sold in retail stores are available only in standard sizes, as listed in the box below. Since our poster is not a standard size, just putting it in a standard frame will not work. However, by adding a mat, we *can* utilize a standard frame. Let's say the poster is 18½ x 23¾". By introducing a mat with side borders of 2¾" and top and bottom borders of 3⅛", we can make the matted poster fit into a frame of 24 x 30"—a standard size, and the most economical way to frame this odd-size art.

As the example above has shown, using a mat broadens your access to standard frames. But this flexibility does not come without a price. Being able to read a $1/16$" ruler is required. Readers who are rusty on reading such a rule have lots of company. You should consult the "Reading a Ruler" box for a refresher course, and you will soon know your way across any ruler.

STANDARD FRAME SIZES

5 x 7"	9 x 12"	16 x 20"	22 x 28"
8 x 10"	11 x 14"	18 x 24"	24 x 30"
8½ x 11"	12 x 16"	20 x 24"	24 x 36"

READING A RULER

A surprising number of people are intimidated by a standard 1/16" scale, and for good reason. The imperial system of measurement used in the United States is so awkward, it has been largely abandoned by the rest of the world in favor of the metric system. But you must be able to read this scale if you are going to do your own picture framing. Here's what you need to know.

On a 1/16" ruler, 16 tiny dashes, called increments, fall between inch marks. The whole system is based on dividing these 16 increments in different ways. For example, if you want to find 1/2", divide 16 in half. Since half of 16 is 8, any count of 8 increments equals 1/2". To find 2 1/2", go to the 2" mark, then count 8 increments above it toward the 3" mark, which will land you at 2 1/2".

Other examples: To find 3 1/4", go to the 3" mark first; then, since one-fourth of 16 is 4, counting 4 increments above it will get you to 3 1/4". To find 3/4", since one-fourth of 16 is 4, it stands to reason that 3/4" is 3 x 4, which equals 12, or a count of 12 incre-

ments. Since locations on a ruler can be expressed in more than one way, 3/4" is the same as 12/16". Likewise, 1/2" is the same as 8/16", and 4/8" is also the same as 8/16". Now, where did that 4/8" come from? Reading a 1/16" scale by eighths is simply reading it by every other increment and ignoring the rest, counting only 8 increments to an inch. It takes 2/16" to make 1/8"; 4/16" = 2/8"; and still another way of saying 4/16" is 1/4".

But why do we need to know three different ways to read a ruler? Because there are three different types of ruler scales. Some rulers have only 8 increments between inch marks; they are called 1/8" scales; some have only 4 increments between inches; they are called 1/4" scales; some have 16; they are 1/16" scales.

To locate any 1/8" measurement on a 1/16" scale, just double the number of increments. So 3/8" is the same as 6/16"; 5/8" = 10/16", and so on. It's a little like splitting hairs. But splitting hairs is a good thing when it comes to measuring. The more increments you have, the more precisely you can measure. And being able to read a 1/16" scale is critical to successful framing.

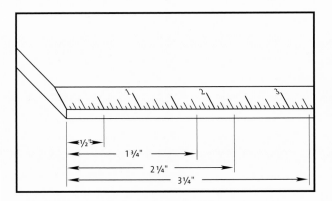

LOCATIONS ON A 1/16" SCALE

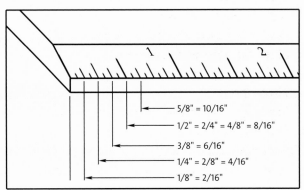

LOCATIONS ON A 1/8" SCALE

To measure for matting and framing, always build from the artwork size outward, not from the frame size inward. So begin by measuring the artwork.

You can use a wooden yardstick if you like, but most have only a ¼" scale and are not very precise. Tape measures are better, although the cloth type are often graduated by ⅛" increments, whereas the metal reel types usually have the ¹⁄₁₆" scale you're after. Most professional framers prefer a metal straightedge rule because it lies flat and provides a hard, straight edge to cut against.

With artwork, the two pertinent dimensions are length and width. But the question often arises: To determine the size of the mat's window, should you measure the image itself or the paper that the image is on? Well, that depends on how you choose to present the image in the mat window. So before you do anything else, you will need to make that decision. When dealing with art on paper, there are three possible choices: bleeds, floats, and art on carrier paper.

BLEEDS

First, let's consider artwork that has an image that takes up the whole sheet of paper. With no blank area surrounding the image, it spreads to the edges of the sheet, or is said to "bleed" off the edges. When picture framers mat a bleed, they try to reveal as much of the image as possible in the mat window, but they usually don't reveal all of it because doing that would require making the window the same size as the paper—in which case, the paper would just fall through the window. To address that situation, the picture framer makes the window slightly smaller than the paper, with the beveled window edges overlapping the edges of the paper to support it. The amount of overlap at each edge is usually ¼", which translates into ½" at each dimension.

In picture framing, it's best to think in terms of dimensions, rather than edges. On any rectangular two-dimensional item there are four edges, but only two dimensions: length and the width. On a mat's window there are four edges, but if we think in terms of dimensions, we realize that there are only two edges to each dimension. If we intend to make the window smaller by ¼" on each edge, then the window will be smaller by 2 x ¼"—or ½"—on each dimension. So if the paper is a ¼" smaller on each edge, it's ½" smaller on each dimension. To determine the window size for a bleed, all you have to do is subtract a ½" from the length of the paper, and ½" from the width, and that's the size of the window. Example: If the artwork is 18 x 24", the window size is 17½ x 23½".

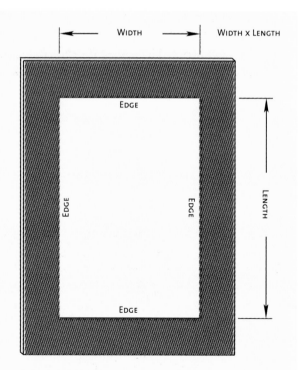

MAT WINDOW

A mat window has four edges, but only two dimensions: length and width.

THERESA AIREY
Gas Pumps

BLEED. To reveal the image only, the window is made slightly smaller than the paper, so that the beveled edges of the window overlap the edges of the paper.

THERESA AIREY
Gas Pumps

MATTED FLOAT. The matted float has the virtue of revealing the edges of the paper within the window of the mat.

THERESA AIREY
Gas Pumps

CARRIER PAPER. Art on carrier paper can be matted to reveal the image and a portion of the blank area surrounding it.

FLOATS

The second way to deal with art on paper is by "floating" it. It's the simplest way to mat something, because you avoid cutting a window at all. Just reduce a mat to the size of the frame and attach the artwork to the face of the matboard. Many photos, particularly, are presented that way. Because the means of holding the artwork is hidden behind the image, the artwork appears to be suspended against the face of the mat, or "floating" there—which is why it's referred to as a *float mat.* When artwork is floated against a mat and placed in a frame with no further embellishments, it is known as a *simple float.* But when a second mat, a window mat, is placed over the floated artwork, with the mat window being larger than the artwork, it is referred to as a *matted float.*

Since a matted float has the virtue of revealing the edges of the paper within the window of the mat, it is often used to present artwork based on a paper quality that contributes to the presentation. For example, art rendered on hand-made paper is often presented in a matted float so that one may enjoy the deckled edges of the sheet. With paper that is characteristic of the composition, such as a Japanese painting on rice paper or an Egyptian hieroglyph on papyrus, the matted float is a sound choice.

To measure for a matted float, first you must decide how much of the under mat you are going to reveal along the edges of the paper and within the window of the over mat. There is no hard-and-fast rule here, but it's interesting to observe how we approach things if we choose to reveal ¼" along each edge. Assuming we have artwork of 18 x 24", and thinking in terms of dimensions rather than edges, to reveal ¼" along the edges of the paper within the window of the over mat, we would have to make the window larger than the paper by ½"

on each dimension. In other words, the window for a matted float of this kind would be 18½ x 24½"—just the opposite of what it would be if we chose to mat the same artwork as a bleed.

Now you can see the importance of determining how you will present the artwork in the window of the mat, since your decision has a direct bearing on the size of the mat window.

CARRIER PAPER

Besides bleeds and floats, there is a third possibility for presenting artwork, designed for images that do not bleed to the edges of the paper. Instead, a blank area of paper surrounds the image. In the printing of posters, for example, the paper that carries the image is called the carrier sheet, and the blank area surrounding the image is the unimprinted, or excess, carrier paper.

Art on carrier paper can be matted as a bleed or floated, but it can also be matted to reveal the image and a portion of the blank area surrounding it. In terms of measuring, this is the simplest proposition of all since you have only to measure out and write down the area you want to reveal in the window; that is the size of your mat's window. But there is one thing you need to be aware of. The next step in the measuring process will have you adding mat borders to your window size to bring you to a frame size. Be sure the borders are wide enough to accommodate the excess carrier paper you are putting behind them. Otherwise, you may end up having to trim the artwork to make it fit behind the mat, and as a general rule, you want to avoid trimming artwork.

To review our procedure so far: Decide how you want to present the artwork in the window of the mat; measure your artwork; then work out the appropriate window size. Now you are ready for the next step.

LOOKING GOOD, SAVING MONEY AND TIME

Selecting serviceable mat borders is a critical part of the measuring process, since by adding mat borders to the window size, you will arrive at a frame size. Always remember: You want a frame size that meets your objectives—one that works for you in terms of aesthetics, economics, and efficiency. Let's take these one at a time.

BORDER FINDER

To find a good starting border for your mat, add the length and width of the window to get the "United Inches," then read across the row to find the border.

WINDOW SIZE IN UNITED INCHES	STARTING BORDERS
9 to 12"	1½"
12 to 24"	1¾"
24 to 32"	2"
32 to 36"	2¼"
36 to 44"	2½"
44 to 50"	2¾"
50 to 54"	3"

AESTHETICS

You will want mat borders that look right for whatever size window you're planning. Borders that are too narrow or too wide may diminish the overall appearance of the piece. (To assist you in selecting proper borders, use the "Border Finder" on this page as a guide.)

To use the "Border Finder," determine the sum of the length and width of your mat window. The two dimensions added together are the "United Inches." For example, the sum of an 8 x 10" is 18". In the "United Inches" column, find the range into which that 18" window falls. Then read across to the "Starting Borders" column to find the size suggested for its mat.

There is only one number represented in each column, because at this point, we are assuming all four borders will be the same. We will soon get to the question of having a deeper, or weighted, bottom border. Note that we call these "Starting Borders" because they will likely not be the ones you end up with. You will probably modify them to satisfy budget and efficiency, but you can rest assured that by consulting the "Border Finder," you are starting with borders that will look correct, and marginal modifications will do no damage to the aesthetics.

Continuing with the example cited above, if our artwork is 18 x 24" and we want to present it as a matted float, the window size will be 18½ x 24½". The united inches are 43" (18½ + 24½), suggesting starting borders of 2½".

SAVING MONEY

If you want to economize, your goal is to acquire a good frame at a low price. Frames in full-inch sizes are generally less expensive than frames measured to fractions. For example, a frame of 24 x 30" will cost less than a frame of 23½ x 29½", because frame suppliers, even those that make custom frames, anticipate a certain demand for full-inch sizes and can prepare for them. But fractional sizes are nearly limitless and can hardly be anticipated, so most have to be made to order. Whenever possible, modify your frame sizes to bring them to full-inch measurements by altering your mat borders accordingly.

Bear in mind that each dimension has two borders, so if your mat window is 18½ x 24½", and the borders are 2½", the frame size will be a nasty 23½ x 29½". To get rid of the fractions and bring the frame size up to a nice even 24 x 30", all you have to do is add ½" to each dimension—which means adding a ¼" to each border.

So, to achieve a frame size of 24 x 30" for a window size of 18½ x 24½", modify your borders to 2¾", and you've got it. Moreover, in this particular case, there's a bonus. The size you've arrived at is a standard size, giving you even greater flexibility in your frame choices and moving you closer to real efficiency.

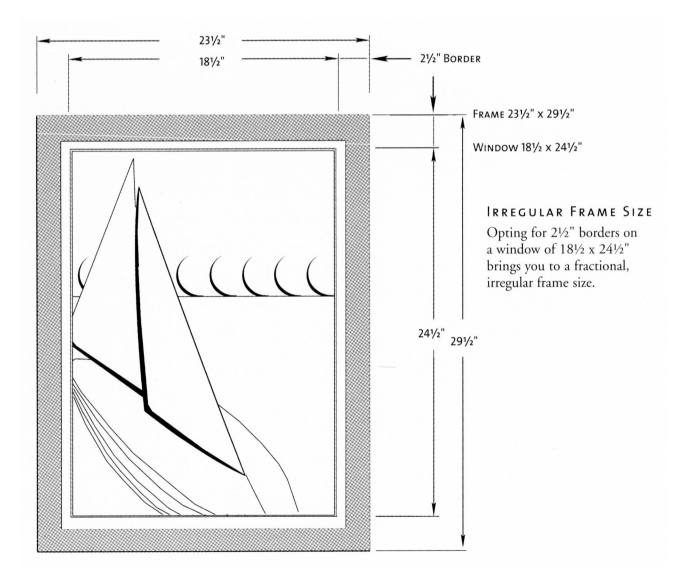

23½"

18½"

2½" BORDER

FRAME 23½" x 29½"

WINDOW 18½ x 24½"

IRREGULAR FRAME SIZE
Opting for 2½" borders on a window of 18½ x 24½" brings you to a fractional, irregular frame size.

24½" 29½"

Saving Time

Efficiency in picture framing is defined by eliminating needless tasks. By purchasing your picture frames already assembled, you eliminate the task of putting them together yourself. I know that many people want to make their own frames, and that topic will be explored in detail shortly, but for others, framing inexpensively with the least amount of toil has the most appeal. So it's worth emphasizing that standard-size frames provide the greatest efficiency, as well as a good price.

If you're not going to make your own frames, there are three ways to buy them: at a frame shop, which is needlessly costly; from a framing wholesaler that sells to the public, which is generally a pretty good deal; or off the rack, already assembled by a mass merchandiser (or sold in pieces that are easily put together).

In each case, there are advantages and disadvantages, but if saving time is your goal, buying frames off the rack, already assembled, may seem attractive.

There is one problem, however. Preassembled picture frames come in standard sizes only, so if you intend to buy them off the rack, you will have to measure everything to standard sizes, and that's not as easy as it looks.

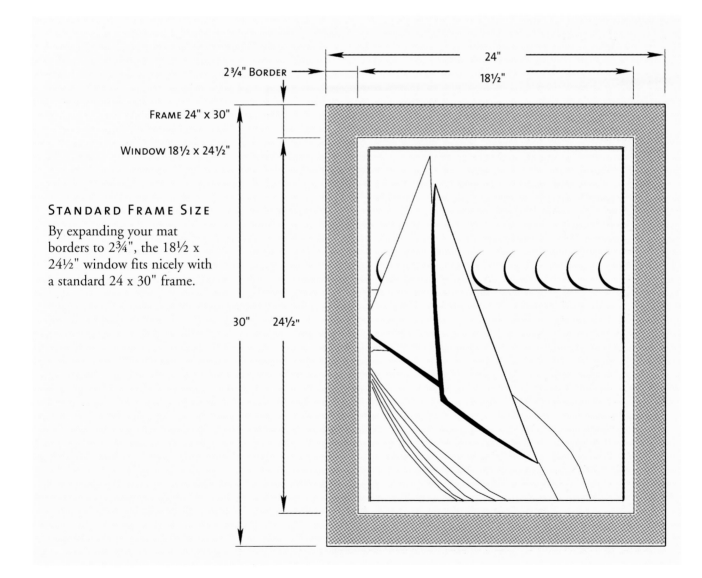

Standard Frame Size

By expanding your mat borders to 2¾", the 18½ x 24½" window fits nicely with a standard 24 x 30" frame.

BEWARE: STANDARD SIZES DO NOT CORRELATE

Let's suppose you have something simple to frame: an 8 x 10" photograph, itself a standard size. The image is oriented as a portrait (which is usually vertical), so 8" is the width and 10" is the height. Suppose we want to put this photo in a frame of a standard size. The natural choice would be 11 x 14"— a standard size offered in precut mats, with a window cut to 7½ x 9½" for an 8 x 10" bleed. We should fully expect that this photo will fit this frame, with the use of a mat, particularly, since both components are in standard sizes. But will it?

To figure the mat borders, subtract the width dimension of the window from the width dimension of the frame. That difference is the amount of space remaining out of which to make mat borders. Since the borders on either side of the window must always be the same, you must now divide the difference in half to find the borders. In our case, that means subtracting 7½" from 11" to get 3½", then dividing it in half to get left and right mat borders of 1¾". Repeating the procedure for the height dimension, 9½" from 14" = 4½". Divide that in half and you have top and bottom borders of 2¼" each.

Considering that we are fitting standard-size artwork to a standard-size frame, you might expect that the top and bottom borders will also be 1¾", but if you add 1¾" borders to 9½", you'll get a frame height of 13", not 14". Why? Here's the surprise: A standard 8 x 10" image is not proportional to a standard frame of 11 x 14", because most standard sizes do not correlate. So you cannot simply fit art to a frame by uniformly expanding or contracting all four borders. Instead, even with a standard-size image, you will have to compensate for the difference in proportion. You can do it in one of two ways: using balanced or weighted borders.

HOW TO CALCULATE BALANCED MAT BORDERS

	WIDTH (INCHES)	HEIGHT (INCHES)
Bleed artwork	8	10
Mat window	7½	9½
Mat borders	(left) 1¾ (right) 1¾	(top) 2¼ (bottom) 2¼
	To calculate mat borders, width: subtract mat window from frame: 11 minus 7½ = 3½. Divide in half: 3½ divided by 2 = 1¾	To calculate mat borders, height: subtract mat window from frame: 14 minus 9½ = 4½. Divide in half: 4½ divided by 2 = 2¼

Is It Better to Have a Weighted Bottom Border?

To summarize the problem: With 1¾" borders on the top and bottom, you don't have enough mat to fill the 14" dimension of the frame; you need more mat. The easiest thing to do is to add an extra inch to the mat's bottom border, making it 2¾". The bottom border is therefore deeper than the top. It is said to have weight. Thus, framers call it a weighted border mat.

Curiously, many artists have been taught that having a weighted bottom border is preferable to making all four borders the same. When pressed, however, most art teachers who espouse this "rule" have only a vague idea of the rationale. Many try to explain it by saying that artwork ought to "sit down" in a frame and have a "base." This would certainly make sense for landscapes. But what about still lifes? Figural art? Abstract art? Do they all benefit from "sitting down" in a frame? Clearly the rule does not apply in all cases.

Another flawed rationale asserts that when artwork is hung above eye level an optical illusion makes the image seem to be falling toward you. Therefore, you must make the bottom border deeper to offset the illusion. This theory assumes that even if all artwork is hung above eye level (which is not the case), it is all hung at the same degree above eye level (again, not the case), and, of course, eye levels differ according to human height. Nevertheless, as ridiculous as the theory is on the face of it, it does have a grounding in fact.

Back in the nineteenth century, when ceilings were higher, it *was* fashionable to hang art high above eye level. In addition, frames were suspended away from the wall, on a long wire, so that viewers had to look up at the image tilted toward them.

Because the art was viewed at an angle, an optical illusion did occur that could be corrected by using a weighted border. But that was in the past. Why does a preference for weighted borders persist to this day?

HOW TO CALCULATE WEIGHTED MAT BORDERS

	WIDTH (INCHES)	HEIGHT (INCHES)
Bleed artwork	8	10
Mat window	7½	9½
Mat borders	(left) 1¾ (right) 1¾	(top) 2 (bottom) 2½
	To calculate mat borders, width: subtract mat window from frame: 11 minus 7½ = 3½. Divide in half: 3½ divided by 2 = 1¾	To calculate mat borders, height: subtract mat window from frame: 14 minus 9½ = 4½. For weighted bottom: 2 at top, 2½ at bottom

Why Weighted Borders Prevail

In short, weighted borders save picture framers time and money. It may come as a surprise to learn that many frame shops do not cut their own frames. Cutting frame moldings accurately is anything but a sure thing, and the cost of waste can mount up quickly. Therefore, many shops source out the cutting job to a local frame wholesaler, taking advantage of what is called a "chop service." Because the wholesaler services many shops in the vicinity and has plenty of volume, it is invested handsomely in highly precise, state-of-the-art equipment for miter cutting and chopping, allowing picture frames to be cut accurately with minimal waste. The frame shop simply calls the wholesaler, orders the size and style it wants, and the order is delivered the next day, relieving the frame shop of the cost of waste.

As a result, the frame shop has very little finished frame stock on hand—perhaps only a few styles in standard sizes. Suppose a customer selects a popular frame style, but the shop has it only in a standard size that won't work for the customer's art. Does the shop immediately call the wholesaler? No. It reminds the customer of the aesthetic preference for a weighted border. The customer recalls having heard such a thing and green lights the idea. The frame shop is happy and the customer is happy. So the thing that's truly driving the preference for weighted borders is not the aesthetics, but the expediency. Weighted borders give the picture framer the ability to fit non-proportional art and frame together using a mat. And it can do the same for you.

Although the foregoing example called for a 2¾" bottom border, that border is quite a bit deeper than the 1¾" top border. Arguably, the weight is too much and risks disturbing the viewer's eye. We can achieve a more pleasing weight by subtracting ¼" inch from the bottom border and distributing it on the top border. So, if we want a bottom border of 2½", we must have a top border of 2", to go along with our side borders of 1¾". Interestingly, even though that 2" top border is larger than the 1¾" side borders, the difference is not too noticeable. But the bottom border is still noticeably larger, but not excessively so, making for a pleasing weight and a fine presentation.

Best Approach, on Balance

Of course, a weighted border is not the only option. As shown in the framed example and calculation table, you could divide the additional inch needed and distribute it in equal amounts on the top and bottom borders. The left and right borders become the same, they balance each other, as do the top and bottom borders. But the two sets of borders have different measures. This method is called a balanced border mat. Interestingly, as long as the two sets of borders are not too different, the overall impression is that all four borders are the same. Hence, balanced borders are a great way to create a sense of balance and harmony when things don't exactly fit.

To summarize, because art often fails to respect the parameters of full inches and standard sizes, and because, even if it does, there is not always a proportional correlation between standard sizes, those who want to achieve efficiency and economy by purchasing preassembled or full-inch frames will find themselves using balanced borders quite often, probably more often than they use mats with four identical borders.

THERESA AIREY
Rice Paddies in Schuan, China

Artwork presented in a weighted border mat.

THERESA AIREY
Rice Paddies in Schuan, China

Artwork presented in a balanced border mat.

BEST PLAN: PLAN AHEAD

At the outset of this chapter, I began by declaring it a mistake to buy a frame before you do your planning. Yet, I have now demonstrated two quick, easy methods to make artwork fit into a frame, so you can be forgiven if you conclude that the problem is not so daunting as it at first appeared. To be sure, you may feel yourself giving in to the allure of garage-sale frames again, but be careful. Just one change to the scenario leads to a costly and time-consuming dead end.

Let's suppose that instead of an 8 x 10" portrait, you have a 10 x 8" landscape. Width is now the long dimension. What happens if you buy an 11 x 14" frame for it? The artwork is still not proportional to the frame size, but now you won't have the option of using a weighted border to fix it, because the weighted part would be on the side.

You could employ balanced borders, but you may not be satisfied with the result, because balanced borders are usually most effective when the top and bottom are deeper than the sides. When arranged the other way—top and bottom borders narrower than the side borders—the appearance tends to disturb the eye.

So, will your 11 x 14" frame bought for an 8 x 10" landscape have to be replaced by an 11 x 13" or a 12 x 13" to make things look right? Don't speculate. You may wind up with unusable frames that will probably make an appearance at your own garage sale at some point. Instead, plan carefully on paper before you buy anything.

CAREFUL MEASURING: A MUST

Many paintings or photos will not fit into standard-size frames without some compromise to aesthetics. Some hobbyist framers are willing to sacrifice aesthetics in exchange for the economy and efficiency offered by preassembled frames. But if you are not in that group, be aware that there are plenty of low-cost, high-quality alternatives offered by mail order and internet frame suppliers.

Nevertheless, you may still want the convenience of purchasing your frames off the rack at a mass merchandiser. If you do, be sure you make informed choices, not hasty ones resulting from poor planning.

Proper measuring is central to good planning. With that in mind and reviewing the procedures detailed above, now you are ready to:

- Decide how you want to present the artwork in the mat window.
- Measure your artwork and calculate the correct window size.
- Select appropriate mat borders, using "Border Finder."
- Modify borders to reach a frame size guided by aesthetics, budget, and efficiency.

The planning stage is nearly complete. The next step will take you to a different realm, an alternate universe where the world of equations and increments gives way to a place of sensibility, where there is no single right answer, where art and framing become one in the wonderful world of color.

SARAH BACCI
Grace in Repose

The image at the top of the page has narrower side borders. The same image, below it, has wider borders on the sides, which tend to disturb the eye.

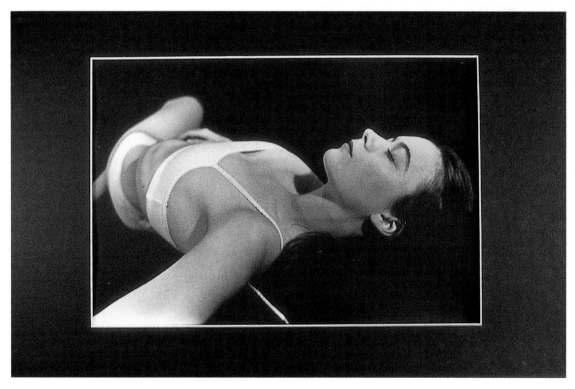

MARY MARK, POEMS ART PUBLISHING
Art framed with Nielsen molding and Bainbridge Artcare matboards.
Photo by Peter Paige, compliments of NielsenBainbridge.

SELECTING
COLORS FOR
MATS & FRAMES

Where will the picture you frame hang? That decision impacts on the colors you select for your mat and frame. Aesthetically, your most basic objective in framing is to enhance the artwork, to draw the viewer's eye into the composition. But paradoxically, if a piece is headed for a juried exhibition, when it comes to presenting work to be judged, your purpose is to make the mat and frame as inconspicuous as possible so that jurists may evaluate the artwork on its own merits. Curiously enough, if the framer's contribution enhances the artwork, it might be considered cheating in a juried show. Therefore, many such shows restrict mats to off-whites and neutral tones, and frames to unadorned moldings. This type of presentation is known as *academic framing*.

On the other hand, when you frame for private display to enhance existing room decor, you will likely shun anything too bland. So if room decor is your guiding purpose in selecting artwork, that purpose should also guide your framing choices.

COLOR BALANCE

It is often said that the framer should respect the artist's intention when choosing colors. While that is a commendable aim, it may be misconstrued to mean that the framer should imitate the balance and degree of colors in the art. Thus, if the composition is primarily yellow or gold, the framing should be primarily yellow or gold. But if art dominated by yellow is surrounded by a yellow mat and frame, it becomes excessive and probably distorts the artist's intention. Instead, the framer should seek to balance colors in the composition with colors in the framing, by selecting a secondary color in the art to act as the dominant color in the framing. Whenever a mat is present, the mat, which should be wider than the frame, provides that dominant color. Begin by taking a good look at the composition, seeking the artist's guidance in selecting a mat color.

HONORING THE ARTIST'S COLOR VALUES

First, consider the dominant *value* of the artwork: the degree of lightness and darkness, ranging from white to black. When it falls more toward white, it's a tint; more toward black, it's a shade; gradations in between are called tones. If the art primarily contains tints, such as a botanical print or a light pastel painting, select a secondary color from your list that is also a tint. If you choose a secondary color that is a shade, you could end up with a fine balance between the framing and the composition, but an inadequate enhancement of the artwork.

So simply cross from your list all secondary colors that don't share the dominant value of the artwork.

ALTOON SULTAN
Laundry Day

Left, a white mat and colorless, unadorned frame characterize the academic framing that surrounds this hand-colored drypoint artwork.
Right, for private display, the objective is to enhance the artwork with the color, texture, and style of the framing.

THERESA AIREY
Stephany by Pond

Left, a mat chosen to pick up the dominant color in the painting produces
an excess of one color, distorting the artist's intention.

Right, this mat picks up a secondary color in the art that agrees with the
painting's dominant value and temperature to balance and enhance the art.

COLOR TEMPERATURE

Next, narrow the field further by crossing off all colors that don't share the the color temperature of the art, that is, the predominance of either cool or warm colors. Cool palette colors are blue, violet, and green; the warm ones are red, orange, and yellow. Which secondary color reflects the temperature of the art?

The choice may not be an easy one. When we talk about the predominance of cool or warm colors, we mean not just the quantity of the color, but the relative importance of the color to the overall meaning of the piece. Often the focal point of the composition is not the point that provides the greatest preponderance of color and yet it is clearly where our eye is meant to go, as in the case of portraits.

HONORING THE FRAMER

Picture framing is an art form. As such, it cannot be reduced to formulas. At some point, your own sensibilities as a framer come into play. The exercise of identifying the art's secondary colors and then eliminating some until you've narrowed your choices can take you most of the way, but it can't take you all the way home. Now you must stand back from the art and ask yourself, What is it about? How can my framing enhance what this work is trying to say?

Coming out of the first stage of planning, which is all rules and equations, the novice picture framer is often surprised at the capriciousness of color selection. There is a tendency to look for formulas and pat answers, but the only answer that will ultimately satisfy is the one provided by you. This is an unsettling notion to the mind that enjoys mathematics and measuring, almost as daunting as the idea of splitting sixteenths is to the creative mind, but what is most difficult for anyone taking up picture framing for the first time is not the adamant nature of math, or the ethereal world of aesthetics, but the fact that they must turn from one to the other in the course of the same project. Engineers build structures. Poets capture feelings. Picture framers do both.

Is White Always Best?

When it comes to choosing a mat color, you may have heard, "White is safest." Indeed, many picture framers look to white, thinking that it is solid and certain, but this thinking can be misleading. First, white is not always the best choice, and when it is, the framer is still faced with an array of options. In their product lines, matboard companies offer more than thirty different hues of whites, some running toward peach, others toward yellow or gray. So if you use a white mat, which white should you choose? Apply the strategy that you used when choosing a color, but instead of looking for a secondary color to act as the dominant hue in your framing, identify the dominant color in the art and look for a white that reflects it. For example, if gold is dominant in the art, choose an off-white with a slightly yellow tone; if blue is featured in the art, pick a white with a grayish cast. Intensity of the white is another factor to consider. For artwork that does not have great color intensity, such as watercolor, it would be a mistake to mat it with an intense white. Since the objective is to direct the viewer's eye into the artwork, the brightest white should come from the art, not from the mat. To choose a white mat for a watercolor, identify the brightest white in the painting, then select a white that is a tone down from it.

When to Use Color

Lighter colors augment a sense of projection in a composition, so contemporary art with bright splashes of color is enhanced by white matting. On the other hand, darker colors tend to augment a sense of recession in a piece. A traditional painting of a Hawaiian sunset, for example, is enhanced by a dark gray or black mat; a white mat might actually work at cross purposes in this case. White is also not the best choice when a composition is already composed largely in whites; a white mat may be excessive—so choose color instead.

Double Mat Color

When double matting, the mat that lies on top provides the broadest area of color. The undermat is usually seen as a narrow band of color around the inside of the window. Since we know the eye travels from white to color, the favored use of color in a double mat is to have a white mat on top and a color mat underneath. This method draws the eye into the artwork. Employ the strategy for selecting white that is detailed above, then select a secondary color for the undermat that matches the dominant value and temperature of the art.

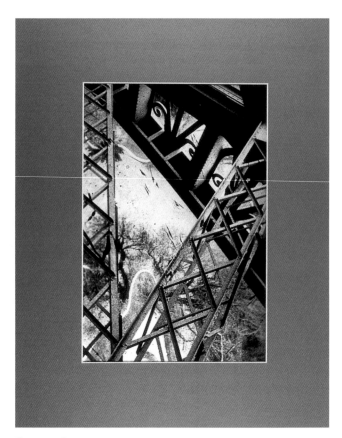

Sally Alatalo
Eiffel Tower
Color matting does little for contrasts in a black-and-white photo; rather it tends to draw the eye away from the composition.

SALLY ALATALO
Eiffel Tower

White matting helps to amplify contrasts in a black-and-white photograph,
which is why many camera artists choose it for displaying their work.

A ccents, such as patterning in the mat or details in the frame, need not have any definite tie-in with colors in the artwork. The same is true of mat cores--the base material of the mat--be they bleached white, cream, or black.

METAL FRAMES come in primary colors, so your selections can coordinate with artwork hues. But having already selected mat colors, you may want to opt for something more conservative when it comes to a metal frame, lest you end up with too many colors and run the risk of a motley presentation. Metal frames of black, silver, or gold are most common. Of them, black creates the clearest boundary against the wall and the least conspicuous statement about the art. Gold confers a sense of luxury. Silver has a streamlined, modern quality.

WOOD FRAMES are a different matter. Largely unavailable in primary colors, they nevertheless present the framer with a choice of hues and textures, from the warm luster of cherry wood to the coarse rusticity of pine. As a starting point, weigh the style and impression of the piece. Is it elegantly traditional? Boldly modern? Warm and fuzzy? Hard-nosed and gritty? Find a frame that fits the mood. A gold frame ornamented with scrolls and foliage says elegance. A black lacquer frame with gold fluting is modern. Honey-finished pine is warm and simple. Distressed wood speaks of ruggedness. Often the composition has wood depicted in it: trees clustered by a field; a tabletop; a wharf. Pick up on the wood that's already there and amplify it.

PREVIEWING RESULTS

To visualize how a frame will look on your art, here, retail frame shops enjoy an advantage, having a selection of frame corners to place next to your art for a preview. Without access to frame corners, consult color pictures of frames in catalogs, or request small frame sections from mail-order frame suppliers. Most customers don't request them because suppliers don't go out of their way to publicize their availability, but ask, and you may be accommodated.

As for visualizing how a mat will look, use a color chart, also called a color specifier, which contains small swatches of mat face papers. They will offer an accurate sampling of available mat colors, but charts do not let you visualize the mat on the artwork; matboard corners do that. These L-shaped sections of matboard can be placed over the corner of your art to let you see how the mat and artwork go together. By stacking them, you can visualize double mat combinations before you cut them. Unlike frame corners, reserved for pros, matboard corners are available to the general public through on-line and other sources.

Sample frame sections from mail-order frame suppliers help you to visualize how a frame will look with your art.

Samples courtesy of American Frame Corporation.

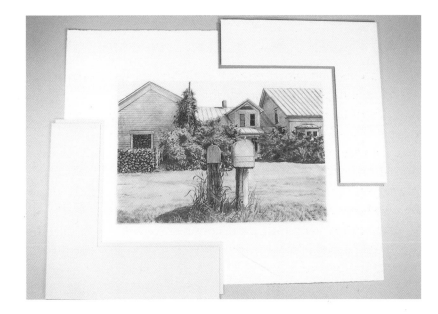

ALTOON SULTAN
Mailbox, Ryegate, Vermont

Matboard corners allow the framer to visualize different mat possibilities before making a choice.

FEELING COLORFUL: PSYCHOLOGICAL RESPONSE TO COLOR

Pink prison cells are a current trend, and unruly inmates are increasingly likely to find themselves in such a setting. This rosy approach is rooted in sound psychological/physiological theory. Pink, scientists tell us, has a weakening effect on physical strength, inhibiting the release of brain chemicals that trigger aggressive behavior. So pink cells make sense. But what if a prisoner is in a red cell? Red affects the pituitary gland, releases adrenaline, sends blood pressure up, quickens breathing, and increases the appetite. So red prison cells are a bad idea.

What do these interesting findings have to do with picture framing? Plenty. A part of your job as a framer is to make color choices that reflect the mood of the work to be framed. While artists have many expressive tools at their disposal—subject, composition, colors—the framer has only color and ornamentation. So choices are critical, and to make good ones, having an understanding of the psycho-physiology of color is beneficial.

For example, suppose the art to be framed conveys a sense of impending trouble—a gathering storm, painted in grays, blacks, and dark blues, with streaks of yellow. Taking your cue from a secondary color, you might choose blue in the frame package to complement the art. But that choice considers only the technical presence of blue in the picture, ignoring its overriding mood. Blue would not be a good choice because its cool nature produces a calming

effect, at cross-purposes with the subject's mood. A better choice would be yellow. Human beings have a precautionary response to yellow; it sends a warning, as in a gathering storm. Thematically, it ties in. But what about its balance with the artwork's overall palette? If yellow dominates the frame package, it would be loud and overbearing. Instead, a cream-colored mat with a yellow hue, combined with a black frame, would make a powerful statement of impending doom and balance nicely with color in the art—adding up to a choice that has depth and meaning.

To cite some other examples: Use brown to frame that picture of a deer in his forest domain; brown suggests security. Green also stimulates a sense of well being—as soothing as a walk in the woods to replenish the psyche. Combine the calming effect of blue with orange to evoke the placid feeling of viewing a sunset.

Industry has exploited the effects of color on human behavior for some time. Food companies that spend millions on packaging know that red promotes appetite; blue reduces it. Government is also sold on the psychology of color. When officials want us to be alert and watchful, they use yellow (caution signs, school buses); to tell us that a resting place is nearby, they use brown (park or recreation-area signage); to get us moving, red is chosen, usually accompanied by a siren. So what makes sense in your color choice? Feel it out.

POSTER ART, BRUCE McGAW GRAPHICS

Art framed with Nielsen molding and Bainbridge Artcare matboards.

Photo by Peter Paige, compliments of NielsenBainbridge.

STEP
·3·

CHOOSING MATERIALS & EQUIPMENT

The first challenge you will encounter in shopping for framing supplies is the plethora of choices that confront you. Should you glaze with glass or acrylic? Use museum-grade matboard, cotton-core, or regular grade? Work with preassembled frames or sectionals? Choose spray adhesives or mounting tapes? A point driver or a brad pusher? A miter box or a power miter saw? To make our way through this labyrinth to sound economical choices, we'll divide items into two broad categories: materials and equipment. Materials are items that you use up in one frame job or over the course of several. Equipment refers to tools that are bought once and used over and over again.

We'll begin by reviewing materials, which break down into two subcategories: regular materials and archival, or conservation, materials. Archival materials are items that promise to safeguard your artwork from damaging elements in the environment, particularly acid and ultraviolet radiation. Every category of material, except frames and hardware, offers at least one choice that is archival. Let us begin by exploring the choices offered in matboard.

MATERIALS: MATBOARD

The function of a picture mat is to separate glazing from artwork and to prevent damage to art from moisture condensation. Because the mat generally touches the artwork, which once caused great consternation in the framing community, echoes of such concern are still heard in the form of apprehension over the archival quality of materials being used.

HISTORY OF MATBOARD PROBLEMS

Early matboard was nothing more than sign board pressed into use for framing artwork. It was simply a board with a wood-pulp core and a white paper lining. In its natural state, wood has lignin in it, therefore, paper made of wood also contains lignin. Unfortunately, when lignin is subjected to sunlight and humidity over time, acid can pass out of it—and into any product that touches it. At the point of contact, a shadowy brown stain occurs called *acid burn.*

When early matboard was used primarily to make signs, such acidity was not a major concern. But with fine artwork, if the mat cannot enhance its longevity, it should at least not subtract from it. To the chagrin of professional framers, the potential of matboard to have this deleterious effect was discovered. It was some time before the impact of what was happening was felt, because acid burn can take up to twenty-five years to manifest itself. When its damage finally became obvious, professional framers were confronted by angry collectors demanding to know what had been done to their artwork. The framers turned to matboard companies for a solution. What they came up with was a *cotton-core matboard* that was not made of wood pulp, but of cotton fibers, containing little or no lignin.

Yet, discovering that artwork had been ruined after years of hanging innocently on their walls made many framers gun-shy. Particularly those with the most to lose, such as museums or collectors framing expensive original art. It was pointed out that the acid problem was not just that it seeped into whatever it touched directly; its contamination was so pervasive that the acid could migrate through all kinds of barriers. While matboard manufacturers contended that such a migration could take decades, even a century, museums were still concerned. After all, their artwork needed to be protected for many hundreds of years.

In addition, protesters pointed out that cotton-core matboard was not entirely lignin-free. While cores were now made of cotton, face papers laminated onto the core to give it color and texture might still be made of wood pulp. Acid could still migrate from the face paper, contaminate the cotton core, and eventually harm the art.

IMPROVED MATBOARD COMPOSITION

But matboard manufacturers were a step ahead of the protesters. By putting the face papers through a bath of calcium carbonate, they were able to balance the pH, neutralizing the acid content in face papers. While they still contained acid, it could do no harm—at least not until acids floating freely in the air assaulted the matboard—which, they pointed out, could take a very long time.

Cotton-core matboard; note the bleached-white core.

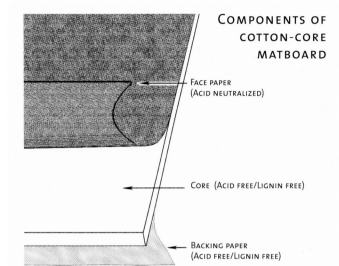

COMPONENTS OF COTTON-CORE MATBOARD

FACE PAPER (ACID NEUTRALIZED)

CORE (ACID FREE/LIGNIN FREE)

BACKING PAPER (ACID FREE/LIGNIN FREE)

Museum-grade matboard; note the bleached core and neutral-colored facing paper.

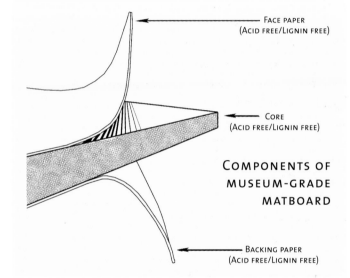

FACE PAPER (ACID FREE/LIGNIN FREE)

CORE (ACID FREE/LIGNIN FREE)

COMPONENTS OF MUSEUM-GRADE MATBOARD

BACKING PAPER (ACID FREE/LIGNIN FREE)

Regular matboard; note its cream-colored core.

COMPONENTS OF REGULAR MATBOARD

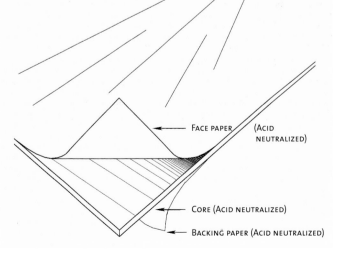

FACE PAPER (ACID NEUTRALIZED)

CORE (ACID NEUTRALIZED)

BACKING PAPER (ACID NEUTRALIZED)

MUSEUM-GRADE MATBOARD

Many museums were still unsatisfied. What they wanted was a matboard that was 100-percent lignin- and acid-free through and through, and also promised protection against free-floating acids in the air. Once more the matboard companies were there with an answer: a matboard made of cotton facing papers over a cotton core. Then they put both through a neutralizing bath of calcium carbonate to erect barriers against acids in the air. The result, museum-grade board, offers the highest degree of protection in a matboard product, but it is quite pricey: about four times the cost of regular matboard.

Do you really need expensive museum-grade matboard to protect your artwork? Possibly not. Even regular matboard provides some degree of protection against acid. Unless you hang your artwork in direct sunlight or in a damp basement, exacerbating the problem, there is little threat of acid contamination from regular matboard in the short term. If you've seen artwork from the 1970s framed with regular matboard that has turned brownish-gold, a sure sign of acid contamination, understand that many manufacturers only started neutralizing regular matboard in the 1980s. Today, regular matboard is improved, although its degree of protection is not as thorough as cotton-core boards. But the difference in effect can be measured in multiples of decades, not months or years.

MODERN MATBOARD CHOICES

So today we have three types of matboards: *regular, cotton-core* and *museum-grade,* available in nearly two hundred solid colors plus dozens of versions that simulate marbles, precious metals, and other specialties. Now there are at least five basic core colors—regular cream core, stark-white cotton-core, bleached-white "white core," and black core—plus many colored cores for special effects.

Since the core color becomes the exposed bevel when the mat is cut, having it available in different hues adds another color element to the overall presentation. For example, a mat having green face paper and a regular cream-colored core cannot say "Christmas" as well as a green mat with a red core. With products from at least four major matboard manufacturers, it all adds up to a staggering variety from which to choose. Where do you begin?

You will find that 90 percent of the mats you use will consist of a few whites and off-whites, a gray or black, and a handful of primary colors; the rest will be selected from the myriad of other available hues. Your own gleaning process will simplify things quickly, and when the day arrives that you simply must have that certain shade of Guatemalan Rusty Rose, you'll be happy to find that a matboard company probably has it.

Matboard comes in two sheet sizes. The vast majority is sold in a 32 x 40" size. The larger sheet, 40 x 60", is considered oversized and rarely needed. A great selection of matboard can be found at art-supply stores and through catalogs and internet suppliers specializing in framing materials.

Many core colors are available. Although subtle, the accent a core color adds through its bevel can also be quite expressive, as in the four core colors shown here: cream, stark white, black, and red.

FOAMBOARD

For backing artwork, filling out a frame, and creating matting effects, foamboard is chosen for its versatility and strength. Light but sturdy, rigid but smooth, and soft enough to be sewn through for object box framing, it is the backing board of choice among pros and do-it-yourselfers. It comes in three thicknesses: ⅛", ³⁄₁₆", and ⅜". (If those sizes seem arbitrary, consider them in their metric equivalents: 3mm, 5mm, and 10mm.) The ⅜" is used for model and stage-set building. In framing, the ⅛" and ³⁄₁₆" are used almost interchangeably, although the thicker is favored for larger framed pieces (24 x 36" and up). The thinner is chosen when the combined thickness of framing components (glazing, matboard, artwork, foamboard) is an issue.

Regular foamboard is not, strictly speaking, acid-free; it has a bit of acid in its core, although nothing like the acid-laden content of corrugated cardboard, foamboard's predecessor in the frame shop. While the threat of acid burn from regular foamboard is not severe, if you are concerned, take measures against it by inserting a barrier sheet of cotton-based drawing paper between the artwork and the foamboard, or use acid-free foamboard, which is laminated with a cotton facing paper.

Unlike matboard, foamboard is marketed in several sizes: 20 x 32", 24 x 36", 32 x 40", 40 x 60", and 48 x 96". Most framers prefer using 32 x 40", to keep it the same size as a standard sheet of matboard. Foamboard is sold through stores, catalogs, and internet suppliers of art and/or framing materials.

Foamboard is a versatile product with many uses for picture framers, which include backing artwork and filling loose space in the components within the frame.

VERONICA SEBASTIAN POTTER
Apples

The blond frame and pale-green inset of its balanced double mat picks up the subtle tones of this painting's secondary colors, allowing the focal point of the art, the bold red of the apples, to hold the spotlight.

GLAZING MATERIALS

The purpose of glazing in picture framing is to protect artwork from dust and other airborne pollutants. To some people, the word *glazing* is just another way of saying that we are using glass, but glass is not the only clear-sheeted material available to place over artwork. Other options follow our discussion of glass.

GLASS

REGULAR GLASS is an alkali-silicate, sodium-lime, 2.5mm single-strength window glass. The word *regular* is commonly applied when this glass is used for picture framing. It is made by heating sand and soda to over 2,000 degrees Fahrenheit, then it is passed over a roller onto a flattening table and put through an annealing oven to make it less brittle, but glass always remains somewhat brittle, making fragility its biggest flaw. In addition, it is quite heavy as compared with acrylic glazing (discussed below), and more prone to moisture condensation. But glass is inexpensive, not easily scratched, and almost universally available—so regular glass remains the preferred glazing method for most picture framers.

NONGLARE GLASS is about twice the cost of regular glass. Glare, those bright swatches of sunlight that obstruct the view of artwork, is banished from nonglare glass by way of a light etch cut in the surface of the glass. The etch makes the glass look cloudy when held up over empty space, but when brought close to the artwork, clarity returns. Nevertheless, some framers are convinced they lose clarity through nonglare glass and reject it for this reason. Others disagree. While the debate goes on, you need only decide how much of a problem glare is for you and whether you want to pay extra to be rid of it.

UV-PROTECTIVE GLASS is a third choice. It is an archival-quality glazing that promises to cut out about 98 percent of the ultraviolet rays that threaten to fade and yellow your artwork. Weigh the importance of protection against ultraviolet radiation versus cost, because this option will cost about four times as much as regular glass. While there is no doubt UV-protective glass does what it says it does, be aware that regular glass is often considered sufficient to protect artwork that is not hanging in direct sunlight or under fluorescent lights for a prolonged period of time.

Regular glass comes in full-size sheets. The largest is 48 x 84", or it can be cut to order, a good option for novice framers. Hardware stores, paint stores, craft shops, and home-improvement centers carry glass, and most will cut it to size while you wait. Specify regular glass for framing, and furnish the frame size.

For photographers and other artists who work in standard sizes, still another option is available: glass sold stacked in presized panels in a quantity equaling 50 square feet. These lites, as they're called, come in standard sizes. The number you get depends on how many it takes to make 50 square feet. For example, if you want a stack of 8 x 10" lites, you would get 90 of them; for a stack of 24 x 36" lites, you would get only 8.

ACRYLIC

Another material for glazing artwork is acrylic, which many people refer to by the brand name Plexiglas. Acrylic has some definite advantages over glass, as well as some distinct disadvantages.

For framing large pieces, say 24 x 36" or larger, acrylic is favored for its light weight. It is also preferred for shipping artwork, as it is virtually unbreakable. But in one sense, acrylic is more fragile than glass, because it scratches easily, and is often sold with a light-blue film over it to protect it from scratches in transit. The film is easily peeled off to reveal the clear, scratch-free acrylic beneath. But be careful handling it. Even something as harmless as

Known as lites, stacks of glass precut in standard sizes are a good alternative for framers who work regularly with the same standard sizes.

a paper towel can cause light surface abrasions in acrylic.

Acrylic should be cleaned more often than glass, using a soft cloth and nonabrasive cleanser suited to plastics. Its vulnerability to scratches is not its only shortcoming. Since it carries a high static charge, even more than glass, dust is drawn to it.

For this reason, acrylic should be avoided when framing artwork rendered in a loose medium such as pastel or charcoal. Also avoid hanging acrylic in direct sunlight, as heat can cause it to buckle or bulge, and if you object to glare, acrylic is not a good choice. You could buy nonglare acrylic, but first you'd have to find it. Frame shops are the only retail establishments likely to have it, and you will pay about three times the cost of regular glass for it.

Acrylic panels used for framing often come faced with a removable blue film to protect against scratches in shipment.

The cost and variety of frames available to you depends on how you go about acquiring them. If you make your own frames, you will enjoy the lowest possible cost but be limited, at least initially, to simple, manageable molding styles. If you buy frames off the rack at a mass merchandiser, prices will be good but choices limited to a few styles and standard sizes. Buying from a mail-order or internet frame supplier offers a better selection and more attractive prices, but still not the tremendous variety your local frame shop offers. For that great range, you will have to get your frames from where the frame shop gets them—at your local frame wholesaler, usually found through your yellow pages under the heading "Picture Frames, Wholesale."

WHOLESALE PURCHASING

Why not just buy all your frames through a wholesaler? Because, in most cases, wholesalers resist selling to the general public, fearing it may undermine relations with their main clientele, retail frame shops. Also, in our system of taxation, only the last person in the distribution chain has to pay sales tax, which absolves the wholesaler of that responsibility; the retailers handle taxes. The wholesalers must keep a record of each of their customers' retail-tax identification numbers. So when you call your local framing wholesaler seeking to do business with him, the first thing he will do is ask for your retail-tax identification number. If you don't have one, he won't sell to you.

But there's a way around this problem, if the variety of frame moldings sold at wholesale prices is compelling enough to make you grapple with a few obstacles. In most states, it is not difficult to obtain a retail-tax identifcation number. It's usually a matter of filling out a simple form. Call your state's revenue office and the form will probably be mailed to you. Fill it out, send it in, and within a week or two, you'll have your retail-tax ID number. Now you can call up your local framing wholesaler and start buying frames.

However, after about three months, you'll get a reporting form from your state's revenue office, asking what you sold and the amount of tax you collected. If you didn't sell anything and only used the molding to make frames for yourself, you will still have to pay what most states call a "use tax," applied to items you buy at wholesale and use for yourself. The rate is generally the same as other local sales taxes, and is figured by estimating what you would have sold the item for, had you sold it. That's the tax you will owe to the state. All things considered, if you frame only a dozen pictures a year, it may not be worth the bother—and the penalty for noncompliance can be unpleasant. But there is another way, as noted earlier, to access a great variety of frame styles at favorable prices, once you know how to go about it.

MAIL-ORDER/INTERNET PURCHASING

Mail-order and internet frame suppliers are not simply shops that have put out print catalogs and websites. Rather, they are picture-frame wholesalers just like your local wholesaler, but with one important difference. They have decided to risk the disfavor of local frame shops in return for the rich rewards of selling direct to the public nationwide. Consequently, they offer picture frames to the public at wholesale prices. If you happen to have a retail-tax identification number, make this experiment. Compare the cost of similar frames bought from a mail-order supplier versus a local wholesaler. Be sure that you are comparing apples and apples. Your local wholesaler will offer the frame in a variety of ways: in length, chopped, chopped and routed, or joined. Frames bought through catalogs or internet suppliers will come to you already assembled ("joined") or in sections ready to be assembled without tools ("chopped

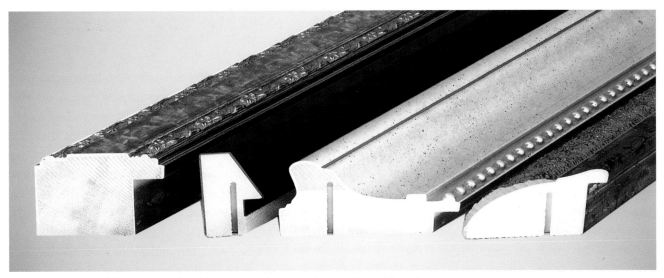

A fine selection of frames is offered by mail-order suppliers at favorable prices.
Photograph courtesy of American Frame Corporation.

and routed"). By comparing like items, you will discover that catalog/internet suppliers and local wholesalers charge about the same.

BUYING MOLDING IN LENGTHS

What about commercial molding sold in lengths? Isn't that cheaper? It is, and it is stocked in eight-foot lengths by local wholesalers, an alternative that you cannot pursue through mail-order suppliers, since it is difficult and costly to ship such long pieces. Also, if you buy molding in lengths, intending to cut and join it yourself, you will need to own a good power miter saw and bench (about $350); a top-quality 80-tooth carbide blade (about $50); corner clamps or a miter vice (about $50); a set of touch-up inks (about $35); and the competence in wood working to avoid a long learning curve and the resulting waste. In short, you must be prepared to make a substantial investment in equipment and training that will probably not be compensated for in the short term by the savings to be enjoyed by purchasing molding one length at a time, which may be one reason why most retail frame shops don't cut their own frames.

On the other hand, if you were to purchase enough stock so that your entire order equaled 250 to 500 feet of molding, you would receive price breaks that would brighten your break-even picture. But you would have to do a lot of picture framing to justify such a large inventory investment. However, there is another way to realize substantial savings by making your own frames, and that is by making the moldings yourself instead of buying premade commercial moldings in lengths. That strategy will be covered in Step Four, "Preparing Materials." For now, I emphasize again that if you want to buy premade commercial moldings, the most economical route is through

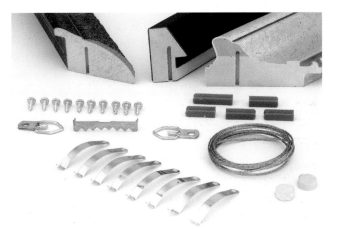

At no extra charge, the essential hardware furnished with a mail-order frame includes strap hangers with D-rings, sawtooth clip, spring clips, hanging wire, bumper pads, and screws.
Photograph courtesy of American Frame Corporation.

mail-order or internet suppliers. When you order from them, you simply furnish the dimensions and style of the frame you have selected. Everything you need to join and secure the frame will be included at no extra cost. The only tools you will need will be a screwdriver and a hammer. Will you be sacrificing something in terms of variety? Doesn't the local wholesaler offer more choice? Perhaps, but you can rival his selection by acquiring as many catalogs as possible. These companies do not duplicate each other's stock, so the more companies you deal with, the broader the inventory you have to choose from. (A list of several firms will be found in "Resources" at the back of this book.)

YOUR BEST BET

A final word about mail-order/internet frame suppliers versus local retail stores. While retailers often offer a framing service, catalog/internet firms will not be of help if you get into a bind—so to prevent problems, it's in their best interest to provide you with a completely satisfying do-it-yourself framing experience. Thus, their catalogs are thorough in providing you with the information you need to make sound choices. Their shipment will include all the hardware you need to complete your frame job. Frames bought in retail stores, on the other hand, provide almost nothing in the way of information and, at least as far as ready-made wood frames are concerned, leave you to fend for yourself in the area of hardware for securing the contents or hanging the frame.

SELECTING A WOOD FRAME

If you make a mistake when purchasing a wood frame, you will probably not be aware of it until you get near the end of the frame job, at which time it will be terribly frustrating to have to start over again. So it behooves you to shop carefully to avoid common pitfalls.

First, realize that when you buy a frame, the size of the frame refers to its inside, not outside, dimensions. It is the interior recess, the part that contains the components, that identifies frame size. For example, a frame marked 16 x 20" refers to the measurement of the recess where you put the matboard, foamboard, and glass: 16 x 20". The overall, outside dimension of the frame will be somewhat larger, depending on the width of the frame face and its ornamentation, but that size need not be of concern, since your main consideration will be to fit the components into the frame.

FRAME RABBET

Having said all that, your main concern in fitting the frame will most likely not be the length and width of the recess but its depth. Don't assume that all frame recesses are the same depth. A frame recess is what professional framers call the "rabbet" of the frame, and its depth varies from as shallow as $\frac{1}{8}$" to as deep as 2". To avoid the problem of having a stack of components that's too thick for the rabbet and therefore sits above the back of the frame, select a frame with an appropriate rabbet depth. Generally, when a stack consists of regular glass, a single mat, artwork, and $\frac{3}{16}$" foamboard, you will want a rabbet depth of $\frac{3}{8}$". For the same stack that substitutes a double mat for a single, a rabbet depth of $\frac{1}{2}$" is best. A stack that includes spacers to separate the mat from the face of the artwork (for charcoal or pastel) could use a depth of $\frac{5}{8}$" in the recess. If the frame you like doesn't come with adequate depth, there are ways around the problem, as you will learn when you get to "Step 8: Glazing, Installing, & Hanging Framed Art." But if you plan ahead, you can avoid unpleasant surprises.

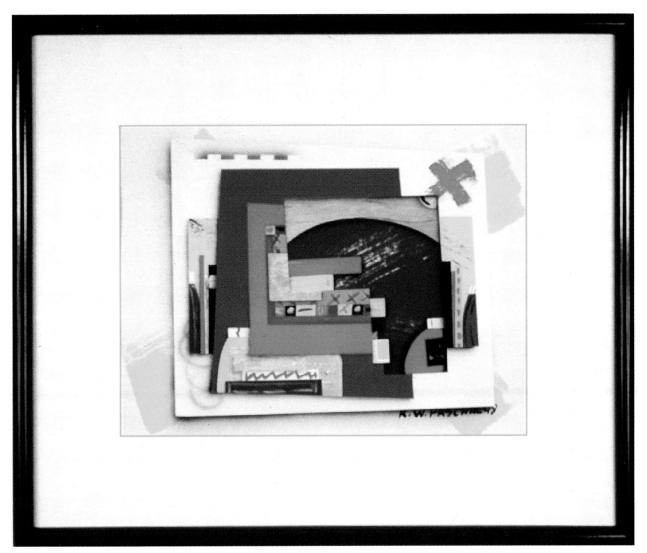

ROBERT PASCHAL
Still Life with TV and Computer Screen

Thanks to the wealth of materials and equipment now available to nonprofessionals, handsome framing like this can be readily accomplished at home by the do-it-yourself framer.

ABOUT METAL FRAMES

When it comes to metal frames, there are pros and cons. On the up side, metal frames are usually easier to work with than wood frames. Assembling them is straightforward and self-explanatory, they require no glue, and everything needed for putting them together comes with the frame, whether you shop at a retail store or through the mail.

On the down side, metal frames tend to be more flimsy than wood frames and may bow under the weight of heavy glass, so it is advisable to use acrylic when framing large items in a metal frame. And note that there is no variation in rabbet depth with metal frames (most are about ⅝" deep), and since the stack of components (backing, matboard, artwork, glass) slides into the frame's extrusion like a drawer, if the contents are too thick, they cannot be loaded. So you should be very careful to check the thickness of your components stack before attempting to use a metal frame.

FRAME FACE AND WOOD TYPE

The width of the frame's face may also be a concern. I once interviewed art jurists about the problems they have with work framed by artists. One of their biggest complaints was that many painters use frame moldings that are either too wide or too narrow for their work. As a rule of thumb, consider frames with a face width of ½" to ¾" for frame sizes up to 12 x 16"; a face width of ¾" to 1" for frame sizes up to 20 x 24"; and 1¾" to 2½" for frames of 24 x 36" and larger.

Finally, consider the kind of wood the frame is made of. Bear in mind that the last step in the framing process is to attach the hanging wire and hardware. When you reach this stage, you will want to be done with the project as quickly as possible, and you may be annoyed to discover that you are unable to screw in the hanging hardware without first drilling a pilot hole. To avoid this hassle, select frames made only of soft and medium-soft woods, such as pine, poplar, and basswood. Steer clear of very hard woods, such as oak, maple, and walnut.

Soft and medium-hard woods will take a wood screw that can be tapped in and secured using hand pressure only. Very hard woods like oak and maple might have much to recommend them in terms of beauty, but require much more of you in terms of effort. As always, making informed choices will prevent unwelcome surprises, especially when they occur near the end of a project.

As a general rule, a wider frame face is better suited to larger sizes of artwork.

Hardwood frames will deny the entry of a hand-turned wood screw, requiring you to drill holes prior to attaching hanging hardware.

A rabbet of ½" depth will accommodate a double mat, glass, artwork, and foamboard backing.

MOUNTING MATERIALS

Mounting refers to the process of attaching artwork within the frame or the mat. Materials for mounting can be categorized under three headings: permanent adhesives, hinge-mounting tapes, and noncontact adhesives.

PERMANENT ADHESIVES

For artwork that can be easily reproduced, such as photographs or commercially printed posters, permanent mounting is preferred because of the flat, firm adhesion it provides. Permanent mounting is characterized by coating the entire back of the artwork with adhesive prior to sticking it down. Do-it-yourselfers most often use **AEROSOL-SPRAY ADHESIVES,** which are easy to apply, readily available, and cheap. However, there are serious drawbacks to spray adhesives. Unless you have a well-ventilated work area (or spray outdoors), the aerosol tends to hang suspended in the air and drift down slowly, leaving a light tackiness on furniture and tools. Another good reason to have good ventilation is that breathing in fumes from spray adhesives poses a health hazard akin to breathing glue into your lungs. so always wear a paper respirator mask when spraying. Also, most aerosol spray adhesives are not repositionable, meaning that as soon as the adhesive contacts the mounting board, it sticks. If you don't place your artwork precisely, you may have a hard time peeling it up to reposition it, at which point the value of having artwork that can be reproduced from a negative or a plate becomes amply clear. However, some spray adhesives are repositionable and state that feature on the can, so read labels when you shop.

Most professional framers use a **DRY-MOUNT PRESS** or a **VACUUM PRESS** for permanent mounting. Dry mounting is wonderfully clean and accurate and poses no health threat. Combining heat and pressure, the dry-mount press bonds prints or posters to the mounting board with the use of a special dry-mounting tissue. The mechanical dry-mount press controls variables of temperature and pressure. The more advanced vacuum press controls time and moisture as well, giving you the most precise and pristine permanent mount available. The downsides of dry mounting have mostly to do with the space and budgetary constraints of the do-it-yourselfer. If you are planning to mat and frame on your kitchen table, these presses are pretty much out of the question. A mechanical press can require a hearty electrical source and many feet of space; a vacuum press can take up the better part of a room, and either can drain your wallet, too. A mechanical press can cost about $900, and a vacuum press can run into thousands.

What most do-it-yourselfers seek is a clean, safe, economical way of permanent mounting that can be done on the kitchen table, if need be. **COLD MOUNTING** provides just such an alternative. Cold mounting is done with adhesive-covered sheets or boards, such as Crescent's Perfect Mount or Seal's Quickstik®. Both provide a rigid cardboard precoated with nonactivated adhesive. The artwork is placed face up on the board. It remains repositionable until pressure is applied by burnishing over the item with a squeegee, at which point the adhesive is activated and the bond becomes permanent. Cold-mounting boards are especially useful for the presentation of matless bleeds, as the board can be trimmed to the print size after mounting. But cold-mounting boards leave much to be desired if you want to float mount. That's where still another option comes into the picture.

POSITIONABLE MOUNTING ADHESIVE, or PMA® as it's called, is a 50-foot-long sheet of paper that comes off a roll and which you cut to a size marginally larger than the print or poster. It comes in three widths: 11", 16", and 24" (from $35 to $60 per roll, depending on width). For artwork larger than 24", the PMA can be appplied in swathes. No seam is apparent when swathes overlap. On one side of the sheet there is a light tackiness. The artwork is burnished onto the sheet image side up. When the sheet is removed, a uniform coat of adhesive remains on the back of the artwork. The artwork is then placed on the mounting surface, be it foamboard or other backing. It sticks lightly to the surface and can be repositioned as many times as is necessary before being burnished down to effect a permanent mount. Like permanent mounting boards, PMA is clean, easy, nontoxic, and provides a flat, firm mount.

Aerosol adhesives are often used by do-it-yourself framers for mounting artwork.

Photograph courtesy of 3M Corporation.

The dry-mount press is favored by frame shops.

Photo courtesy of Hunt Corporation SEAL® Brands.

Cold mounting with Positionable Mounting Adhesive is the do-it-yourselfer's answer to the professional's dry-mount press.

Photograph courtesy of 3M Corporation.

HINGE-MOUNTING TAPES

The adhesive-heavy mounting methods described above are tailor-made for reproducible artwork, such as photographs and posters, but strictly *verboten* when it comes to original art. One-of-a-kind artwork, such as watercolors, pastels, and inks, should be hinge mounted, which is another way of saying that you are mounting your artwork using tape. Household tapes like masking tape or cellophane tape are no good for this purpose, because they carry a high acid content that can threaten your artwork, not to mention the fact that they tend to dry out and let go.

Framing and hinge-mounting tapes are specially designed for artwork. There are a few different kinds offered. The most economical is GUMMED PAPER TAPE, ideal for mounting artwork that is medium to heavy weight. Gummed tape is reversible with water (when you wet the adhesive it releases cleanly) and is acid-neutralized. GUMMED LINEN TAPE is for the heaviest artwork and is acid-neutralized and either self-adhesive or water reversible. MOUNTING/HINGING TISSUE is your best choice for lightweight, transparent art, because it won't show through. It is reversible with mineral spirits. For the highest level of archival mounting, Lineco's Museum Mounting Kit provides you with acid-free, lignin-free Mulberry Paper strips (to make hinges) and a jar of rice starch that you can cook into an organic lignin-free adhesive to brush on the strips before pressing them into service as tape.

Regardless of which tape you use, hinge mounting is accomplished by suspending the artwork with only a few tabs of tape along the top edge. The fewer, the better. One reason for this is to minimize the amount of contact that the adhesive has with the artwork. When it comes to original art, the less adhesive on the artwork, the better. Looked at this way, the third category of mounting might be considered the best from an archival point of view: mounting with no adhesive contacting the artwork at all.

Lineco offers the best variety of tapes for archival mounting of artwork.

NONCONTACT ADHESIVES

Two methods of noncontact adhesives stand out for being easy, clean, and economical. **SELF-ADHESIVE MOUNTING STRIPS** are four-inch-long Mylar strips, divided in half, one half covered with adhesive, the other half adhesive-free. The artwork is positioned on the mounting board and a strip is placed along each edge with the adhesive-free portion overlapping the edge of the artwork. The part with adhesive on it is pressed down against the mounting board while the artwork is trapped by the overlapping adhesive-free portion. No adhesive contacts the artwork. When it becomes necessary to remove the artwork from the mounting board, it's a simple matter of bending back the strips and lifting out the artwork, perfectly preserved.

A variation on the same theme are **MOUNTING CORNERS.** A brand called Lineco Infinity Archival Mylar Photo Corners incorporates and updates the method of corner-trapping used in old photo albums. In this case, the corner holders are Mylar pockets with adhesive on the back. The pockets are adhered to the mounting board, and the corners of the artwork are slipped into them. As with the strips, when it comes time to remove the artwork, it's a simple matter of lifting the artwork out. No adhesive contacts the artwork.

There is one disadvantage to noncontact adhesives. Because they trap the edges or corners of the artwork, they require the use of a window mat to conceal the edges. This means float mounting is not an option if you intend to use a noncontact adhesive.

Whichever materials you choose, your decision should be guided by the type of artwork you are mounting. As I indicated earlier, with artwork such as photos or posters that can be reprinted or acquired again, a permanent mounting method is preferred. If the artwork is an original, one-of-a-kind creation, hinge mounting or a noncontact adhesives should be used. All materials discussed can be found at frame-material suppliers on the internet. A good variety can also be tracked down at art-supply stores, and some are sold in hardware stores.

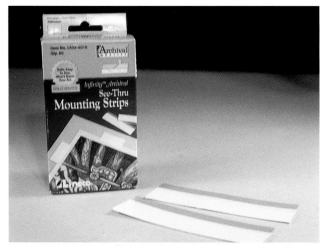

These mounting strips are economical, and easy and efficient to use.

Mylar pockets provide secure corner holders.

HARDWARE

Perhaps the most important ingredient in a picture frame is not the mat, the glass, or even the backing board, for without all of those, the frame can still be hung on the wall. But without a brad or point, a screw eye or strap hanger, and a wire, the artwork doesn't go up, and it doesn't stay up. In picture framing, small things make a big difference, and they are all sold by on-line frame suppliers, most neighborhood hardware stores, and at many art-supply houses.

BRADS are among the most inconspicuous of hardware items. A slender, almost headless nail, brads range from ½" to 3" in length, and are used to nail together the corners of a frame in traditional frame making or to secure the contents of the frame by being inserted into the frame rabbet.

FRAMER'S POINTS are an alternative to brads. A flat metal tab pointed at one end, it is pushed into the side of the rabbet to secure the contents of the frame. The point is driven perpendicular to the rabbet, avoiding the awkward-angled hammering needed to secure a brad, and it effects a tighter pack of the frame contents.

SCREW EYES have a loop at one end of a screw. Used to tie off hanging wire preparatory to hanging, screw eyes can be difficult to attach, particularly on hardwood frames. Moreover, they stick out of the back of a frame and can mar the wall. But there's a good alternative to screw eyes preferred by many picture framers.

STRAP HANGERS, also known as *mirror hangers,* are easier to use than screw eyes and are able to carry more weight. This device is a metal tab with a hole in it and a D-shaped ring at one end. The tab is laid flat on the back of the frame with the D-ring portion overhanging the frame contents. A tapped-in wood screw goes through the hole in the tab and into the back of the frame. Hanging wire is then wrapped onto the ring and stretched across to the opposite D-ring.

OFF-SET CLIPS, also called *mirror clips,* are useful when the stack of components is too thick for the depth of the frame recess. Its Z-shape allows an off-set clip to rise above and overlap the edge of the stack while still being easily attached to the back of the frame with a wood screw.

SAWTOOTHED HANGERS are small metal bars with a serrated edge, used in place of hanging wire and best suited to lighter frame jobs. A particular advantage of the sawtooth is its self-centering quality, allowing you to choose the apex of the serration that results in your artwork hanging straight on the wall.

SERRATED CORNER BRACKETS, known by their brand name Wall Buddies, are a good choice for very heavy artwork. They attach to the back of the frame in each corner, eliminating wire stress and bowing. Made in two sizes, the larger can handle up to 100 pounds of hanging weight.

PICTURE WIRE comes in different sizes and weight capacities. The kind sold at hardware stores for framing is of the smallest size and weight capacity. Picture framers most often use a nonrusting wire capable of holding about 20 pounds of weight. Many favor the use of wire that has a plastic coating, which prevents the unbraiding that results in stinging finger pricks when tying off. Plastic-coated wire with a 20-pound capacity can be purchased through frame suppliers on the internet.

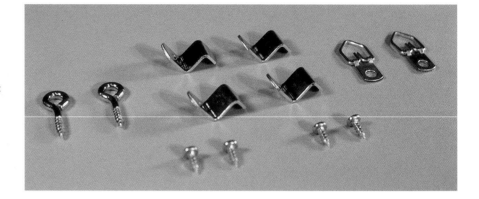

Screw eyes, off-set clips, strap hangers, and wood screws are basic materials for the do-it-yourself framer's tool box.

TRANSFER TAPE

Although not "hardware," **ADHESIVE TRANSFER TAPE** is one of the most versatile and reliable items in the framer's tool box. From holding together double mats to attaching a dust cover used at the back of wooden frames to prevent dust penetration, double-sided adhesive transfer tape is ready and able to do the job. Some of its other uses in framing are to hold together double mats and to tack down curling corners when the artwork warrants such treatment.

But these tapes are not without flaws. They can stick to your fingers, and even with an applicator gun are awkward to handle. Is there an alternative? In a word, no. Nothing bonds as strongly with as thin and uniform a layer as adhesive transfer tape. Rubber cement cannot be applied as neatly, and may discolor over time. Glue sticks lack the requisite bonding strength. White glue can grow brittle and crack under the weight of heavy matboard. All in all, only adhesive transfer tape has the right qualities for matting and framing. But what kind of adhesive transfer tape should you use—and not use?

First, be aware that the double-sided tape sold at hardware stores for laying insulation and carpeting is too thick for picture framing. Another no-no is Scotch 3M Double Coated Tape, designed for attaching single sheets of paper and not strong enough to hold double mats together for a long period of time. For manual application, the right choice is 3M Hand-Held Adhesive Transfer Tape 465. The 3M Adhesive Transfer Tape 924 (called ATG tape) is designed for use in an adhesive transfer gun (thus the ATG). Another brand is Filmolux acid-free transfer tape, for those seeking a completely archival frame job.

Handheld adhesive transfer tape (#465), preferred for its strength and neat application, is a double-sided product made by 3M.

OTHER ESSENTIAL MATERIALS

WOOD GLUE is the simplest, yet most essential material you will need for assembling wood frames. It is the primary bonding agent that holds a wood frame together.

GLASS CLEANER should be kept on hand by the do-it-yourself framer, and the standard product you would use for windows or mirrors will suffice. There are alternative methods for cleaning glass covered later in the book, when we get to glazing and hanging framed artwork, but if you want to simplify things, just pick up a bottle of commercial glass cleaner at the supermarket. If you're working with acrylic, you can find plastic cleaner at your local hardware store.

ESSENTIALS FOR FRAMING NEEDLEWORK OR OBJECTS

If you plan to frame needlepoint, cross-stitch, crochet, or three-dimensional objects, you'll need a few more tools. A needlework blocker, cotton batting, needle-art tape, straight pins, and needle and thread are required for framing needle art.

A needlework blocker is a piece of hardboard with a measuring grid on it, used to restore squareness to a newly stretched needlepoint preparatory to framing it. Cotton batting is used to elevate the needlework off the backing board and promote air circulation through the fibers of the fabric. Needle-art tape is a fast, economical method of mounting needlework. Straight pins are used to stretch and secure needlework to the edges of a mounting board; a needle and thread can be used to stitch it to the board, which is the most popular mounting method. All of these items can be found at fabric stores, craft stores, and internet suppliers of framing materials.

Items needed for mounting three-dimensional objects include invisible thread, a pilot needle, silicon rubber sealer, mounting fixtures, and an attractive fabric, such as velvet or suede. The fabric is used to cover the mounting board, creating a lush background on which to present objects. Invisible thread is used to tie down, support, and drape textiles, the chains of jewelry pieces, or other loose objects. A pilot needle is used to pass invisible thread through the thickness of the foamboard mounting surface. A silicon rubber sealer secures spherical items such as balls; it holds them securely and can be removed cleanly if the object is dismounted. Mounting fixtures are specially designed brackets, each one formed to hold a specific object, such as a knife, gun, coin, plate, or spoon. These devices are found at internet suppliers; silicon rubber sealers at hardware stores; fabric, pilot needles, and invisible thread at fabric stores.

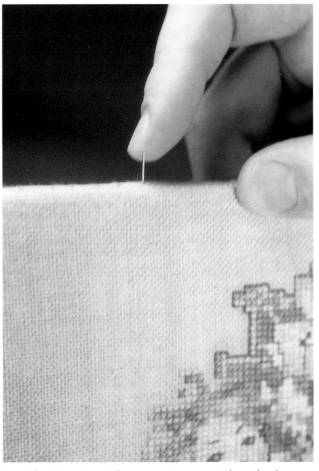

Straight pins are used to secure cross-stitch and other needlework to a mounting board.

OPTIONAL MATERIALS

Two items deserve mention as optional materials, although many framers might consider them essential: dust covers and commercial spacers. A dust cover is made of kraft paper—the brown paper used on the back of a frame. I consider it optional, because you can forgo its use altogether with no adverse effect to the presentation. Regardless of its name, the dust cover is not there only to block dust; it's there as a cosmetic measure, because the packed components seen from the back, as well as the points and brads, aren't all that attractive. Brown paper looks a lot better. If you're framing for yourself, however, you may be the only one who sees the back of the picture, so why go to the trouble and extra cost of covering it up? Of course, if you plan to sell or present a framed piece to someone else, a dust cover will convey a final touch of professionalism.

Kraft paper, also known as "mailing paper," is carried by most stores that sell office supplies and by those that carry arts/crafts supplies. Regular kraft paper is not acid free, but archival-quality acid-free kraft paper can be found at some internet suppliers of framing materials.

As described in an earlier step, commercial spacers separate glazing from artwork and can be used to create shadowbox effects. If a mat is in place, commercial spacers are not essential, and if the framer perceives no great value in the artwork, placing the glazing in direct contact with the artwork is not a terrible risk. However, if the artwork is to be safeguarded or a separation of glazing from artwork is desired for aesthetic effect, commercial spacers are a good choice, available through internet suppliers.

This acrylic mounting fixture, one of several versions, is designed specifically to hold a coin.

Commercial spacers are used to separate art and glazing.
Photograph courtesy of Frame Tek, Inc.

Leaving the area of materials, we now focus on permanent items for your picture-framing arsenal. This equipment needn't be costly or wide ranging. In fact, very few items are considered essential. As defined here, essential means equipment that can lead to an immediate and substantial cost benefit over using outside sources or less-expensive alternatives. There are plenty of other items that may be serviceable, and we'll discuss them as well. But essential equipment for picture framing can be narrowed to just four items: a screwdriver, a hammer, a utility knife, and a mat cutter. By far, the most expensive piece of equipment you must buy will be a mat cutter.

MAT CUTTERS

The trick in purchasing a mat cutter is to get just what you need, no more, no less. Bear in mind that there are two mat-cutting operations to perform: to reduce a full-size sheet of matboard to your frame size; and to bevel-cut a window in the resulting mat blank. All too often, prospective buyers think only about bevel-cutting the window and forget about the need to size the matboard first.

HANDHELD MAT CUTTERS are what many end up buying. Inexpensive handheld cutters (under $50) will bevel-cut a window in a mat, but provide nothing for sizing. Most people who use a handheld cutter end up cutting sheets to size with a utility knife and a straightedge, a time-consuming, clumsy enterprise that quickly leads to burnout. Bevel-cutting a window with a handheld cutter is also no walk in the park. The pressure needed to move the mat cutter along often causes the straightedge to slip. You can clamp the straightedge to a table, but by the time you've gone to that trouble, you might as well have bought a better mat cutter, one that included a straightedge.

A **COMBINATION BEVEL-CUTTING HEAD AND STRAIGHTEDGE** (about $75) offers a cutting head that latches onto the straightedge and any pressure

applied to the head is in turn applied to the straightedge, reducing slippage. But there is no provision for sizing; a utility knife still must be used. Although a straightedge is less likely to slip away from the cutting head, the matboard can slip under the straightedge.

The **32" MAT-CUTTING SYSTEM** (about $95) offers a gratifying alternative. This is the first mat cutter we might properly call a machine. It includes a cutting base that is 32" long on which are fixed a straightedge (now called a guide rail) and an adjustable mat guide that is used as an abutment to reduce slippage further. The system measures borders surrounding the mat's window and does a good job of cutting the window. Some models even include a 90-degree straight cutting head for trimming and sizing. This machine shortens the learning curve and makes it possible for beginners to get the results they desire in a relatively short period of time. But it, too, has its shortcomings.

Handheld mat cutters are inexpensive,
but difficult to use.

On the face of it, the biggest drawback of a 32" mat cutter appears to be its size. After all, a matboard sheet is 32 x 40", so we might conclude that with a 32"mat cutter, large mats can't be cut. But that is not so, because the cutter is open at either end, allowing the matboard to be shifted along the face of the bed to overhang either end for cutting a window of any size. The restriction is the size of matboard that can be put into the cutter for sizing. Since there are only 29½" between the link arms that hold the guide rail, a 32" cutter cannot take a full-size sheet. However, by trimming 3" from the 32" dimension, the full-size sheet can be reduced to 29 x 40" to fit in the machine. Yet, having sacrificed a few inches, reducing the matboard to size with these mat cutters is no breeze. As with a handheld mat cutter, sizing with a 32" cutter requires measuring and marking the full-size sheet by hand before putting it into the cutter for sizing. The next grade of mat cutters purports to solve this problem, but really does not.

The lower-priced of the **40½" MAT CUTTERS** (about $190) appear to be efficient because they provide enough distance between the link arms to accommodate full-size sheets of matboard. But they do nothing to address the issue of marking the matboard out by hand, so after having spent a lot of money to get top-quality features offered by a frame shop, many do-it-yourselfers are disappointed to find themselves still doing something a professional framer would never do: marking out matboard by hand prior to sizing it. Retail framers avoid this by using a tool that every frame shop's mat cutter has: a squaring arm.

A **SQUARING ARM** is key when it comes to sizing. It allows for full-size sheets to be measured and sized at proper right angles without marking out the lines. It makes sizing speedy and accurate and completes the picture of what a full-featured mat cutter should offer: a 45-degree bevel cutting head (for cutting windows); a 90-degree straight cutting head (for sizing); a fixed guide rail; a 40½" cutting board; a mat-guide measuring system for measuring and marking out windows; and a squaring arm for measuring prior to sizing. When you have a mat cutter with these features, you have a complete mat-cutting system.

A combination handheld mat cutter and straightedge helps reduce the problem of slippage while bevel-cutting a mat window.

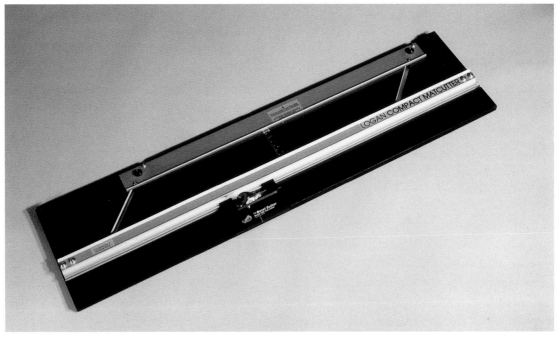

The Logan Compact Mat Cutter is a 32" mat cutter with a guide rail and adjustable mat guide that reduces slippage further.

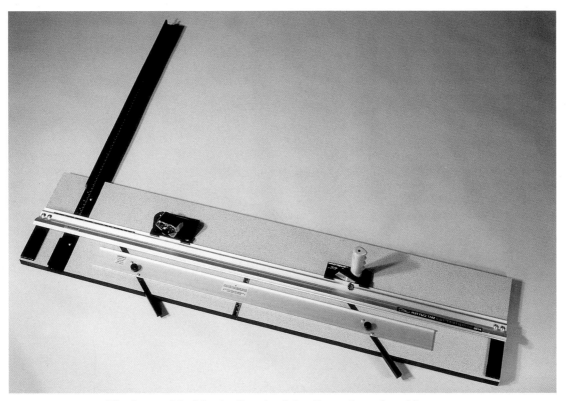

The Logan Model 750 Simplex Mat Cutter is preferred by many professional artists and photographers who do their own framing.

Your Best Bet

The Logan Model 750 Simplex (about $290) is the least-expensive full-featured mat cutter and the number-one choice of artists, photographers, and collectors. There are other full-featured machines that cost more, and often do-it-yourselfers buy them, hoping that by spending more they'll get more and better features—but they end up buying something they'll probably never use. High-end mat cutters, those that cost more than $500, are designed for professional framers and anticipate heavy use, dozens of mats a day. Although they offer little in the way of additional features, they are constructed of heavy-duty materials that can withstand the wear and tear of repetitive use. It is this durability that accounts for the substantially higher price. For the do-it-yourselfer who anticipates cutting only a dozen or so mats a week, an investment in the ability to cut dozens of mats a day is a waste. Higher-end mat cutters should only be chosen if one expects to go into business in the near future. Otherwise, middle-range choices are best for the do-it-yourselfer. A selection of them can be found at better art-supply stores and through internet suppliers of framing materials.

Hand Tools

Some basic hand tools are required for picture framing, but surprisingly few. You will need a utility knife, its quality dependent on the type of mat cutter you use. If you own a full-featured mat cutter, a simple snap-blade knife will suffice, as your mat cutter will do the job for more heavy-duty work. If you use a hand-held mat cutter or a combination bevel-cutting head and straightedge, choose a more heavy-duty tool such as a mat knife (about $10).

If you work only with a handheld cutter, you'll need a good-quality block-edged straightedge to cut against. Some straightedges are beveled along the edge, which is no good; the cutter can ride up over the edge. Many T-squares have a plastic guard along the edge—also no good. The cutter can slip under the plastic guard. For mat cutting, the edge must be blocked so that the cutter has something to ride against. Metal straightedges are usually the best choice (about $15).

Because different types of screws are used in picture framing, you will need both a Phillips-head and regular straight-blade screwdriver. Even if you already have both, a worthwhile investment for picture framing is a power screwdriver, such as the cordless model made by Black & Decker, with a combination regular and Phillips bit (about $35). Remember, in order to avoid the drilling of pilot holes, you will be attempting to screw in your hanging hardware with hand pressure. When you're working with soft woods, it will be easy, but with medium-hard woods, it will be tough. Having a power screwdriver can relieve a lot of grunting and perspiration.

You will also need a hammer. A 10-ounce claw hammer is recommended, but you might experiment with different weights to see which works best for you. If you anticipate using dust covers, consider a nifty device specially designed for the accurate trimming of paper dust covers (about $7). Retail outlets, internet suppliers, and hardware stores carry the hand tools listed above, but go to an art-supply store for a block-edged straightedge.

Tools for Securing Contents in Wood Frames

Your options for securing the contents in a wood frame are many and varied, so you must decide which method you intend to use, and whichever tools you choose to perform the job will be considered essential. Without them, your frame's contents will simply fall out.

For driving, squeezing, or pushing brads, using a pair of needlenose pliers and a hammer is the least expensive but clumsiest method. Pushing with a brad pusher is a possibility, if you confine yourself to soft woods. Utilizing a brad squeezer to vice the brad into the frame rabbet is an option--if you can find one; most hardware stores don't have them. However, the majority of professional framers prefer points to brads, which can be inserted using one of three tools.

The aptly named **POINT PUSHER** doesn't pretend to be anything it is not. A point is fitted into a contoured socket at the end of a curved handle. You grab the handle, put the tip of the point against the rabbet of the frame, and shove. Simple as that. The most popular point pusher goes by the name of the PushMate (about $11).

The Fletcher FrameMaster Point Driver operates easily and neatly with a squeeze of the handle.

A **POINT SQUEEZER**, less crude in operation, is a vicing tool that squeezes the point into the rabbet. It has an adjustable magnetic anvil that holds the point in place. The opposing jaw is fitted over the frame, then the handle is squeezed, closing the jaws and pressing the point into the rabbet. It is called the Fletcher Frame Mate Point Squeezer (about $40).

The **POINT DRIVER** is, without doubt, the ultimate in point-insertion devices. Similar in design and operation to a staple gun, the point driver shoots points perpendicularly, rather than straight down, as would be the case with a staple gun. It operates with a squeeze of the handle and bangs home the point with authority, letting you know that the point is neatly imbedded. You can even adjust the firing tension for different densities of wood. The most popular point driver is the Fletcher FrameMaster (about $75).

Tools for inserting brads can be found at most hardware and woodworking stores. Point-insertion tools can be found at some art-stores and on line at internet suppliers of framing materials.

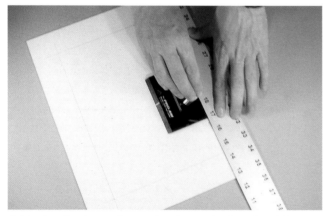

A block-edged metal straightedge is the best kind for matting and framing.

OPTIONAL PERMANENT EQUIPMENT

Some items that may seem like a luxury under ordinary circumstances become essential if you choose to frame in a certain way. Other items that may not be considered important at first become essential later, as your talent grows.

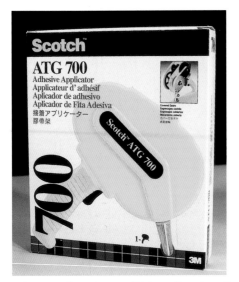

The Scotch ATG 700® Tape Gun is a fine addition to the burgeoning picture framer's arsenal of permanent equipment. Photograph courtesy of 3M Corporation.

The Logan Model #703 V-Groove Cutter can give sophisticated and elegant accents to mats.

A **GLASS CUTTER** is one of the first items you may opt for as you get deeper into picture framing. Largely unnecessary at first, because you will be buying your glass precut to size at a retail store, the utility of a glass cutter becomes obvious the first time you chip a piece of glass. Without a glass cutter, that piece is useless to you. With a handheld glass cutter (about $20), chipped glass can be sized down to be used in a smaller frame.

An **ADHESIVE TAPE APPLICATOR GUN** is another fine item for the burgeoning picture framer. This wonderful tool eliminates the fuss and bother of applying adhesive transfer tape by hand. Often called the ATG gun, a tape applicator gun applies a narrow band of double-sided tape while reeling up the release paper. The most expensive applicator guns (about $45) are the kinds used by frame shops; less expensive models (about $25) also work efficiently.

OVAL/ROUND MAT CUTTERS are for those who want to flex their mat-cutting muscles. A range of such cutters can cost in excess of $800, but a hand tool that offers results on a par with costly machines is the Logan 3-Step Oval and Circle Mat Cutter. It produces ovals from 3½ x 4" to 20 x 23", and circles in a similar range, and costing under $100, is a viable choice for do-it-yourselfers and low-volume professional framers. Operated independent of tabletop models, the Logan 3-Step produces oval/round windows with a 45-degree bevel. Used in combination with a straight-line cutter, unique window designs are possible, such as dome-shaped mats and Victorian windows.

A **V-GROOVE CUTTER** produces the handsome decorative groove sometimes seen on the face of a mat. The V-Groove Mat Cutter (about $100), a tool that works in conjunction with your straight-line cutter to cut two close-set opposing bevels on the mat's surface, produces a V-shaped groove, an elegant and sophisticated accent that speaks volumes about your matting acumen.

THERESA AIREY
City Walkers

This very deep bottom mat border almost seems to be a path that leads the viewer
into the artist's fascinating street scene.

FURTHER OPTION: EQUIPMENT FOR MAKING FRAMES

If you plan to make your own frames from scratch, several large pieces of professional equipment are essential. An accurate **POWER MITER SAW**—not a miter box—is needed to cut and join premade moldings bought in length. Miter boxes are altogether inadequate for making picture frames, and anyone who implies differently is leading you down the primrose path. That's not to say that it's impossible to make frames with a $50 miter box, if you want to fumble and struggle. But an accurate power miter saw can save you hours of frustration. Be prepared to spend about $200 for the saw, plus $100 for a **WORKBENCH** to clamp it to, and $50 or so for an **EXTENSION ARM** to hold long strips of molding while cutting. And don't put just any old circular blade in that miter saw.

An **80-TOOTH CARBIDE BLADE** will provide the highest-quality, finest cut. Be aware that 24-tooth or 40-tooth blades are usually inadequate and will create a ragged cut that requires considerable sanding, causing a visible seam at the joint that will require paint touch-up. Steel blades are less expensive but won't last as long, so for the greatest economy over the long haul, carbide blades are preferred. Be prepared to spend about $60 on the blade.

CORNER CLAMPS are needed for joining the frame; a set of these clamps holds the miters together while you nail them. Figure to spend about $50. Alternatively, you could purchase a **MITER VICE** for about $75.

Having become this heavily invested in cutting and joining the frame, you may want to go further and buy equipment for making your own frame moldings. This is where the real savings lie. To rip lumber stock into narrow strips preparatory to making moldings, a **10" TABLE SAW** will do the trick nicely for about $350.

Your primary equipment for fashioning the frame is a **2-HORSEPOWER ¼" SHANK ROUTER** for about $100. A **BENCH-TOP ROUTER TABLE** is the most economical surface for it: about $65.

For the more ambitious, a heavy-duty combination **INDUSTRIAL PLUNGE ROUTER AND TABLE** provides greater power and versatility for an investment of about $400. It may seem like a substantial extra investment, but given the increased potential in savings, it seems short-sighted to go into framing at this professional level without spending whatever amount enables you to produce fine frames from scratch.

All of the recommended tools are sold by hardware or woodworking stores and home-improvement centers.

Notwithstanding the above section on making frames from scratch, since the thrust of this book is for the great majority of do-it-yourselfer readers who want to work with precut or preassembled frames, the list opposite shows just what you need to spend to get started.

Having acquired the materials and equipment you need to mat, mount, and frame in the way that is most comfortable for you, you are ready to begin the process itself: modifying any oversized or unfinished materials to prepare them for the frame job you are about to undertake.

THE BOTTOM LINE

In the introduction to this book, I promised to show you how to frame pictures without spending a lot for equipment, and I advised that you can buy everything you need for less than $350. Here's how—and note that this is particularly possible if you comparison shop before buying, as you will often find the same item at various outlets with widely differing price tags.

EQUIPMENT PURCHASE OPTIONS

ESSENTIAL EQUIPMENT	APPROXIMATE COST
40½" mat cutter with squaring arm	$ 290
dual-head power screwdriver	35
10-oz. claw hammer	14
utility knife or mat knife	10
TOTAL	**$ 349**

NONESSENTIAL GOOD-TO-HAVE ITEMS	
point pusher	$ 11
glass cutter	20
dust-cover trimmer	7
TOTAL	**$ 38**

TOP WISH-LIST OPTIONAL ITEMS	
point driver (instead of point pusher)	$ 75
adhesive tape application gun	45
oval/round mat cutter	70
TOTAL	**$ 190**

EQUIPMENT FOR FRAME MAKING (OPTIONAL)	
table saw	$ 350
power miter saw	200
workbench	100
router	100
router table	65
carbide blade	60
extension arm	50
corner clamps	50
TOTAL	**$ 975**

MARY MARK

Art framed with Nielsen molding and Bainbridge Artcare matboards.

Photo compliments of NielsenBainbridge. Room setting courtesy of Usona Home Furnishings, Philadelphia.

STEP ·4·

PREPARING MATERIALS

Once you've bought your materials, you'll find that some of them are not yet in the size or shape you need. For example, unless you plan to use a 32 x 40" frame, your matboard and/or foamboard of that standard size will be too large for other jobs and will need to be reduced. If you are going to make your own frame moldings from scratch, you will need to cut and shape your lumber. And to assemble an object box, or shadowbox, you may have to construct the box yourself, if an avilable store-bought box does not suit your purpose. All of these endeavors require careful preparation.

Accurately reducing matboard and foamboard to your frame size can be time-consuming and precarious, or it can be quick and precise. As emphasized in the preceding chapter, it all depends on the tools you use. So let's begin with the equipment recommended to do the best job for sizing matboard and foamboard.

SIZING MATBOARD LIKE A PRO

By far the easiest way to size matboard is to have a 40" mat cutter with a squaring arm. It will take a full-size sheet of board; the squaring arm provides an abutment that keeps it square during cutting; and it has a mat-guide measuring scale.

Working with a 32 x 40" sheet of matboard or foamboard, to find the maximum yield for whatever size you're reducing to, take the short dimension (32") and divide it by the short dimension of your frame. Then take the long dimension (40")

and divide it by the long dimension of your frame. Add the two together and see what you get. Now do the reverse: Take the short side of your frame and divide it into 40; then take the long side and divide it into 32; add together to see if the number you get is higher or lower than the number you got before. The higher number indicates the best orientation of the board for yielding the greatest number of the size blank you desire.

Before sizing, remove the mat guide. Now, following the pictures and captions:

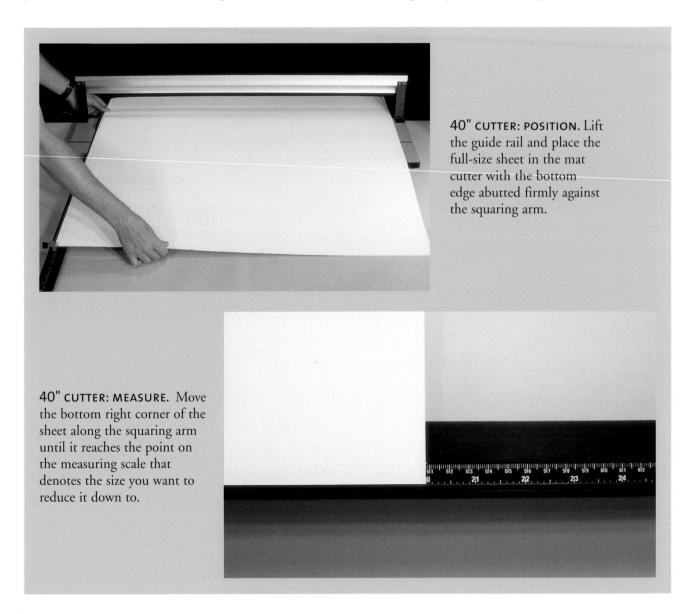

40" CUTTER: POSITION. Lift the guide rail and place the full-size sheet in the mat cutter with the bottom edge abutted firmly against the squaring arm.

40" CUTTER: MEASURE. Move the bottom right corner of the sheet along the squaring arm until it reaches the point on the measuring scale that denotes the size you want to reduce it down to.

40" CUTTER: ONE PASS. Lower the guide rail and put your straight cutting head on the guide rail so the blade is outside the top edge of the sheet. Pressing down firmly on the cutting head, pull toward you, cutting through the sheet in one pass.

Remove the scrap and turn the remaining sheet one-quarter turn. Abut the bottom edge against the squaring arm, measure out the remaining dimension on the scale, and repeat the cutting procedure. Your board is cut to size.

For sizing foamboard, make an adjustment to your blade depth, so that it will cut deeper; adjust it back again to a shallower depth when cutting through matboard.

HOW TO GET THE MOST FROM A STANDARD SHEET OF 32 X 40"

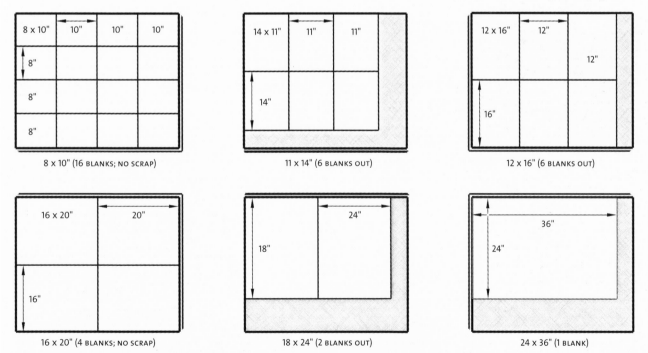

8 x 10" (16 BLANKS; NO SCRAP)

11 x 14" (6 BLANKS OUT)

12 x 16" (6 BLANKS OUT)

16 x 20" (4 BLANKS; NO SCRAP)

18 x 24" (2 BLANKS OUT)

24 x 36" (1 BLANK)

Derive maximum usage from standard sheets of matboard or foamboard by cutting multiples of the same size from it. These illlustrations show the best layouts for obtaining the standard sizes you will most likely need. Saved overage scraps will come in handy for practice cutting and other uses to be discussed later.

Economy Choice: Sizing with a 32" Cutter

When sizing with the 32" mat-cutting system, you must trim 3" from your full-size 32-x-40" sheet, reducing it to 29 x 40" to fit into the machine for sizing. With no squaring arm in this system, boards must be marked outside the machine, then you are ready to size.

Referring to the photos and captions below:

32" CUTTER: POSITION. A sheet of matboard or foamboard that is longer than the cutter can be put into a 32" machine. Because it is not outfitted with a squaring arm, this cutter has no abutment along the ends. Simply let the excess sheet hang out either end.

32" CUTTER: SHIFT, CUT. Cut until you run out of mat cutter, leaving the blade extended into the board, then shift the board back, carrying the cutting head back with it, until you have moved it back far enough to continue the cut.

32" CUTTER: COMPLETE. After marking out the 29-x-40" board, place it in the 32" cutter. Slide the sheet under the guide rail and line up one of the lines you've marked with the edge of the guide rail. Place your straight cutting head on the guide rail and cut, trimming along the drawn line. Turn the sheet and repeat the procedure for the other line.

Although the 32" mat-cutting system is not as sophisticated as the 40" cutter, it does solve most of the problems inherent in using the mat-cutting tool that many novice do-it-yourself framers turn to first: the utility knife. To summarize the advantages of the 32" system: It has a fixed guide rail to prevent straightedge slippage, and because the cutting head can be hooked onto the guide rail, the problem of a wandering blade is eliminated, allowing for one-pass cuts.

SIZING WITH A UTILITY KNIFE

If you do your sizing manually, using a utility knife instead of a machine cutter, your watchwords are: Score, score, and score again. The trick in sizing with this tool is to avoid going too fast. Bearing down on the blade and trying to penetrate the board in one pass will almost certainly lead to a wandering blade, one that diverges from the straightedge, taking its own path. You will have to score your matboard several times before penetrating it; the more, the better.

Play this little game with yourself: See how many times you can score the board before cutting through. The first score is the most important and should be very light, just scratching the surface. Subsequent scores will track on the first score. With each successive score you will be cutting more deeply and following the cut more securely, reducing any tendency for the blade to wander.

After about five or six scores, you should cut through cleanly.

Naturally, when cutting with a utility knife you will employ a straightedge to guide you; it should be made of metal, not plastic or wood, which can be damaged by the blade during cutting. Hold your straightedge firmly, as it will have a tendency to slip. Make sure that the sheet is laid out flat for cutting, and always use a sheet of waste matboard under it as a precaution against cutting into your tabletop.

Cutting foamboard with a utility knife presents other problems to keep in mind. Remember that the soft core of the board is easily gouged out, so twisting the blade even slightly during cutting will result in scoops and scallops. Always keep the edge of the blade parallel to the edge of the board as you cut. Take whatever measures you can to keep the straightedge from slipping; due to the smoothness of its face paper, foamboard has an even greater tendency toward slippage than matboard.

When using a utility knife for sizing, your first score is the most important and should be very light, just scratching the surface. Always use a metal straightedge held firmly in place with hand pressure.

HOW TO SIZE GLAZING

Reducing glass and acrylic is relatively simple and straightforward if you have the right tools. However, it's not a process you want to pursue until it becomes expedient to do so, because storing large sheets of glazing can be a hassle, and handling large sheets of glass can be dangerous.

Therefore, reserve the sizing of glass and acrylic to trimming pieces bought earlier that have gotten scratched, chipped, or broken and are useless until sized down further.

CUTTING GLASS

As with sizing matboard and foamboard, the utility of having a mat cutter with a squaring arm is revealed. With a squaring arm, you simply line up the edge of the glass with the proper measurement on the squaring-arm scale, then cut along the guide rail using the glass-cutting accessory that goes with your mat cutter.

Absent a squaring arm, first tape a sheet of freezer paper to your table. Mark two lines on it, using your straightedge. The first line is where you'll line up the edge of the glass; the second line, parallel to the first, is a distance from it equal to the size you want to reduce your glass to, plus the width of the glass-cutting head.

Place your glass on the freezer paper. Line up the edge of the glass with the first line. Looking through the glass, line up the straightedge along the second line. Using a glass cutter, score the glass. Then part the glass by first tapping it on the underside at one end of the score and then snapping it along a table edge, or use a pair of glazier's pliers to part it.

Always wear cotton gloves when handling glass, not only to avoid smudging it, but also to keep the tiny grains of glass dust off of your hands.

CUTTING ACRYLIC

A mat cutter can be used to cut acrylic; however, there is no acrylic-cutting accessory designed specifically for use with a tabletop mat cutter. Cutting outside the mat cutter, the procedure is simpler than cutting glass, since you can mark lines on the protective paper covering the acrylic and forgo the freezer paper.

As for a hand tool, there is an acrylic knife, also referred to as a plastic cutter, which differs from a glass cutter in that it is equipped with an acrylic blade for scoring acrylic, rather than a glass-cutting wheel for scoring glass.

You will have to score acrylic glazing three or four times to get it to the point where you can snap it. After you've parted the acrylic, you might want to sand away any burrs along the edges. Leave the protective paper on the acrylic sheet until you are ready to frame with it.

MAKING FRAMES FROM SCRATCH

As noted earlier, making your own frames is an option you may wish to forgo. Wholesale sources exist for buying ready-made wood and metal frames of fine quality, miter cut to your specifications, and this book explores how to deal with them. But if you elect to create your own frames, this section is for you.

Of course, when making frames from scratch, you don't actually have to start with the tree; someone will cut it down and mill it into lumber for you. But you will have to select the lumber and shape it into molding. Choose lumber that cuts easily for picture framing. Hardwoods such as oak, walnut, cherry, and maple are beautiful to look at but difficult to cut, so if you are inexperienced at woodworking, you will be better off using softwoods such as pine, cedar, and basswood. Be careful, though; some woods have a tendency to split. Watch out particularly for birch and ash. For beginners, pine and basswood are your best bet because they are soft, easily worked, and resist splitting. In time you can experiment with different types of wood and become familiar with their varying qualities.

LUMBER LENGTHS range from 6' to 14', but 8' is the most common. Several widths and thicknesses are available, but interestingly, the actual size is not the size implied. For example, the size called a "1 x 2" is not actually 1 x 2"; it's ¾ x 1½", because the drying and milling process reduces the original 1 x 2" dimension. This is true of all boards. So remember, if you are going to make a frame with a 2" molding and you buy a "2 x 2" to do the job, that board will actually measure 1½ x 1½". Other common lumber sizes for picture framing are 1 x 2, 1 x 3, and 1 x 4, each smaller than its implied size. Another caveat: Buy only kiln-dried lumber for making frames. Green lumber is cheaper but undried, more difficult to work with, and as your frame dries hanging on the wall, it may shrink or crack.

CONSTRUCTION MOLDINGS can be fashioned into picture frames. Sold by lumber yards, they come most often in lengths of 8'. Base-shoe molding can be turned into a serviceable frame by routing a rabbet along one edge. Base-cap molding is a decorative choice that yields up a handsome picture frame with the routing of a rabbet into its thick end. Basic frame making is largely a matter of routing a rabbet into a piece of lumber. This is true whether you begin with preformed construction molding or with a length of lumber.

Many construction moldings can be fashioned into serviceable picture frames. The types shown are (from left to right) base shoe, cove, and base cap.

CALCULATING LUMBER NEEDS

To determine the length board you need to make a frame, follow these three calculation steps:

For a frame of 16 x 20":

1. Add length + width, then double: 16 + 20 (x 2) = 72"
2. Take width of frame face x 8 + above:
   ¾" x 8 = 6" + 72" = 78"
3. Take thickness of saw cut x 8 + above:
   ⅛" x 8 = 1" + 78" = 79" (or 6' 7")

STOCK TO BUY: 8' length (standard size closest to 6' 7" needed)

STEP 2 acccounts for the miter cut you will make at the end of each section. The number 8 represents the number of times the molding must be cut to make the frame. Since there is a miter cut at each end of each section, and it takes four sections to make a four-sided frame, there are eight cuts in all.

STEP 3 accounts for the thickness of the saw cut (the blade's "kerf," which is usually ⅛"). The number 8 again represents the number of cuts needed to make a four-sided frame.

Box Molding

This most basic of frame moldings is produced by cutting a 1¼" rabbet into a length of 1 x 2 lumber using a table saw. Although the procedure is simple, safety can be a concern because you must remove the blade guard to accomplish it. Always wear goggles and use great caution in operating a table saw without a blade guard. Follow the manufacturer's safety instructions to the letter.

To set up your table saw to cut the rabbet, remove the blade guard and set the fence of your table saw at ¼" from the far side of the blade's teeth. Set the depth of the cut at 1¼". Place your 1 x 2 stock on its narrow edge and flat against the fence. To keep your hands out of harm's way, use something to push the molding forward as you run the stock over the spinning saw. Designed specifically for this purpose and sold at hardward stores, sometimes the device looks like a block, sometimes more like the yellow handle pictured. Now, referring to the photos and captions:

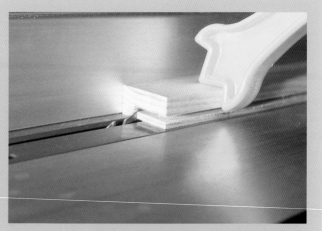

BOX MOLDING: NARROW EDGE. Place the stock on its narrow edge. Using a handle-type push block to hold the wood in place, keep the wood flat against the fence as you advance it over the saw.

BOX MOLDING: WIDE EDGE. After turning off the saw and resetting the fence at 1/4" from the near side of the blade's teeth, set the depth of the cut for 1/4". Lay the 1 x 2 on its wide edge and flat against the fence. You will be connecting this cut with the previous cut, thus neatly notching out a rabbet. Run the stock over the spinning blade using a push block.

BOX MOLDING, COMPLETED. The finished frame is narrow on its face, but deep at the rabbet.

FLAT MOLDING

The flat molding is, for all intents and purposes, the same thing as the box molding but with the rabbet on the narrow edge. This means that the face of the molding will be the wide dimension of the stock. The flat molding is an essential basic molding used as the foundation for a wide variety of styles fashioned with a router. It can be made with a table saw.

The basic steps to follow are shown in the photos and captions below:

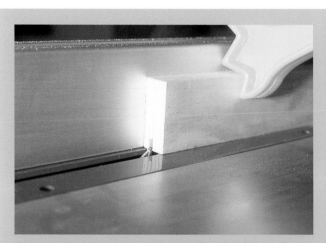

FLAT MOLDING, NARROW EDGE: Set the fence of your table saw at ¼" from the near side of the blade's teeth. Set the depth of the cut at ¼". Stand the stock on its narrow edge and push it flat against the fence. Use a push block to advance it over the spinning saw.

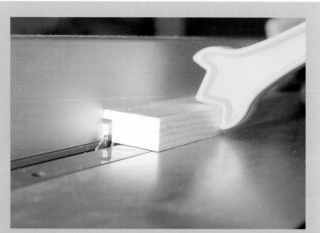

FLAT MOLDING: WIDE EDGE. Reset the fence ¼" from the far side of the blade's teeth. Reset the depth of the cut to ½". Lay the stock on its wide edge with the previous cut nearest to the bottom. Use a push block to advance it over the spinning saw.

FLAT MOLDING, COMPLETED. The finished flat molding is wide on its face.

J-Molding

To make a J-molding, you'll have to move beyond a table saw to a router and table combination. Begin by making a box molding and then turn to your router table. Install a ⅜"-radius round corner bit into your router's collet (metal casing). Adjust it to a half cut. Now, following the photos and captions shown:

J-MOLDING: ROUNDING THE FACE. Stand the box molding on its narrow edge with the rabbet nearest to the bottom and its widest edge against the fence. Advance the stock over the bit, rounding the face. Repeat the process with the bit set for its full ⅜" depth.

J-MOLDING, COMPLETED. After routing, the face is sanded to achieve smoothness.

Coved Molding

To make a coved molding, start with a flat molding, which has the rabbet on the narrow edge so that the face of the molding is the wide dimension of the stock. Install a ⅜"-radius cove bit into your router and set it to rout a depth of ³⁄₁₆". Following to the photos and captions shown:

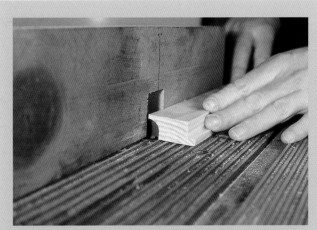

COVED MOLDING: ROUTING. Lay your flat molding on its face with the edge opposite the rabbet pressed up against the fence. Advance the molding over the router, routing a cove into the face.

COVED MOLDING, COMPLETED: The finished cove molding has a smooth concave recess.

Beaded Molding

Again, begin with a flat molding, the rabbet on the narrow edge, the face on the wide edge.

Install a ⅜"-radius beading bit into your router. Set it for a depth of ⅛".

The basic steps to follow are shown in the photos and captions below:

BEADED MOLDING: ROUTING. Lay the molding on its face with the edge opposite the rabbet pressed up against the fence. Advance the molding over the bit. Reset the depth to ¼" and repeat the procedure. Make a final pass at the full depth. Passing a molding over the router in subsequent passes prolongs the life of the motor and avoids damaging the wood.

BEADED MOLDING, COMPLETED. The finished beaded molding has a gentle convex curve.

Beveled Molding

Once again, begin with a flat molding: the rabbet on the narrow edge, the face on the wide edge.

Install a ½" chamfering (beveling) bit into your router. Set it for a depth of ⅛".

The basic steps to follow are shown in the photos and captions below:

BEVELED MOLDING: ROUTING. Lay the molding on its face with the edge opposite the rabbet pressed up against the fence. Advance the molding over the bit. Reset the depth to ¼" and follow the same procedure again. Make a final pass at the full depth.

BEVELED MOLDING, COMPLETED. The finished beveled molding has a clean, angled edge.

SANDING AND FINISHING MOLDING

When making picture frames, sanding and finishing can feel like half the work. Electric sanders are best for rough sanding but in most cases, the job will have to be finished by hand. Sandpaper grit comes in three textures, from coarse to extra fine. Using a sanding block, the best for smoothing unfinished wood moldings is 120-grit (medium) and 220-grit (fine) sandpaper. A set of wood dowels may be needed to get inside the curves and gullies of scooped and rounded moldings. A dusting brush and tack rag are used to remove loose grains of sawdust from the molding preparatory to finishing it.

How you finish the molding depends on how much of the natural color and texture of the wood you want to show through. For wood with an inherent beauty, a protective coat of clear varnish or lacquer will suffice. Use oil stains and water-soluble stains to alter the color of wood. Oil and acrylic paints will mask the original color of the wood, imparting a revised hue. When painting a frame, the wood should be sealed first with several coats of shellac. In most cases, the medium is applied with a brush, but sometimes it may be sprayed on. Obviously, painting does the most thorough job of concealing the original color of the wood.

After you have sanded and finished the molding, you are ready to cut it and join your frame. That process will be covered in "Step 7: Assembling Frames."

EDWARD ALDRICH
Ancient Guardians

The narrow balanced mat and frame bordering this picture strengthen
its powerful image by pulling the eye directly to the elephants.

PREPARING AN OBJECT BOX

To present three-dimensional objects, your frame must be deep enough to accommodate the thickness of the items to be displayed. Sometimes the depth needed is less than 2", but quite often it is not. While it's possible to make frame moldings with a depth of 2" or more, such an enterprise is better left to advanced woodworkers. On the other hand, it may not be easy to find commercial moldings that offer substantial depth in the sizes and styles you need. Consequently, many framers make a separate object box out of wood and fit a frame of standard depth over it, much like placing a lid on a shoe box.

To make an object box, arrange the objects you want to frame on a tabletop. Ascertain the size of the box by figuring the amount of space neeeded to display the objects, taking into account that a mat will encroach on the display area by at least ¼" along each edge. For stock, pine is a good choice; using a 1 x 4 bought at a lumberyard, remember that the board will actually be ¾" x 3½". Saw the board into two pairs of two lengths, representing both dimensions of your box, but be careful; the long sides of the box will have to be 1½" longer than you originally figured because you will lose the ¾" thickness of the wood on either side of the box when you join the ends of the long sides to the inside edges of the short sides, making the interior of the box smaller, unless you account for it.

Following the photos and captions shown:

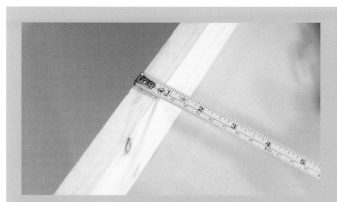

OBJECT BOX: STOCK. The interior of the object box will be smaller by the thickness of the wood used to construct it. The 1 x 4 stock bought at the lumberyard actually measures ¾" x 3½".

OBJECT BOX: PARTING STOP. Nail a rabbet made of a parting stop to the interior of the box. This piece is a cutting of ½" x 1".

OBJECT BOX, COMPLETED. The corners of the box are nailed together; then the outside of the box is stained or painted.

At this point, you have gone as far as you can in preparing materials for an object box. The framing process will resume later in the book in the chapter devoted to mounting.

MARY MACKEY

Art framed with Nielsen molding and Bainbridge Artcare matboards.

Photo compliments of NielsenBainbridge.

STEP ·5·

CUTTING MAT WINDOWS

There is a popular perception that if you can cut a window in a mat, you've mastered the most difficult part of the process. Indeed, assuming that you work with easy-to-assemble frame moldings in a range of styles and sizes and forgo the challenges of cutting and joining frames, cutting a good-quality mat is probably the most difficult part of the process.

It's difficult because it's surprisingly easy to cut a bad mat. Ragged edges, overcuts, and wavering bevels are not uncommon even with the most sophisticated equipment, and if you've handicapped yourself with a hard-to-use tool like a handheld mat cutter, difficulties are practically guaranteed. So the first step to getting consistently good results in mat cutting is to outfit yourself with a decent mat cutter: at minimum, a 32" mat-cutting system; a superior choice would be the 40½" cutter. But understand that a mat cutter is an instrument, not a machine. It will not automatically give you the results you expect of say, a coffee machine. Rather, like a musical instrument, a cutter requires some understanding and skill on the part of its operator.

HOW TO GET GOOD RESULTS CONSISTENTLY

When you cut a mat, a wafer-thin piece of metal is slicing through a highly compressed stack of paper. The different sheets of paper that comprise the stack are called *plies*. Matboard is usually constructed of four plies. Because they are so tightly pressed together, the core is quite dense. That wafer-thin piece of metal is your razor blade, and it will want to flex as it passes through this dense core. If it does, it will show up in your final result as a wavering along the beveled, or sloped, edge of your window, which may reveal itself as a subtle dip or curve on the beveled edge. To prevent wavering and produce a window with consistent 45-degree beveled edges, you must eliminate any undue drag on the blade, because anything that causes the blade to drag will invite blade flex.

USING AN UNDERLAYMENT

A common cause of blade drag is a blade that is cutting too deeply. To prevent that from happening, always place a second mat under the mat you are cutting. This is commonly referred to as an *underlayment,* backing sheet, or slip sheet. Your blade should fully penetrate the mat you are cutting and just scratch the surface of the underlayment. If you cut too deeply into the underlayment,

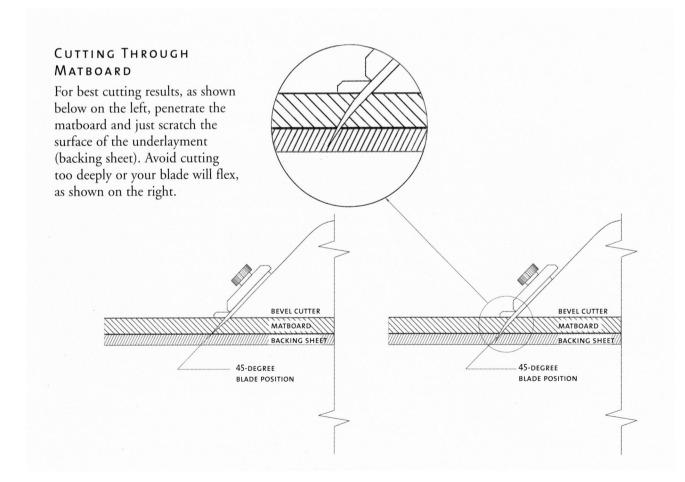

CUTTING THROUGH MATBOARD

For best cutting results, as shown below on the left, penetrate the matboard and just scratch the surface of the underlayment (backing sheet). Avoid cutting too deeply or your blade will flex, as shown on the right.

BEVEL CUTTER
MATBOARD
BACKING SHEET
45-DEGREE BLADE POSITION

BEVEL CUTTER
MATBOARD
BACKING SHEET
45-DEGREE BLADE POSITION

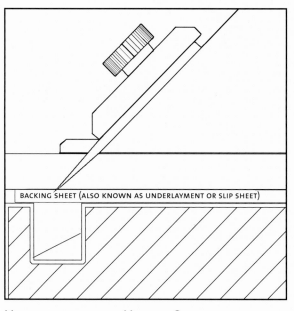

UNDERLAYMENT HELPS CUT

An underlayment, or backing sheet, supports the face paper and promotes clean cuts.

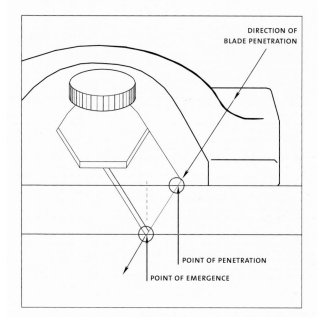

HOW BLADE TRAVELS

Since the blade travels through the mat at an angle, it penetrates the rear of it at a point farther back than its point of emergence in the front.

you will expose too much blade and drag it un-necessarily through the second sheet of matboard as you cut, inviting blade flex. Adjust your blade depth to reduce such unnecessary drag.

An underlayment is any piece of scrap mat-board. One will usually be included with your mat cutter, but when that one gets too scored up, just replace it with any piece you have left from sizing down a larger matboard. It's nice to have an un-derlayment that is as long as your mat cutter's cutting bed, but it really only needs to be as long as the mat you are cutting. An underlayment has two purposes: to protect your work surface, and to give you crisp, clean cuts. The underlayment pro-motes clean cuts by supporting the face paper of your matboard as you cut through it.

Without an underlayment, you will still be able to cut by going into the air space provided by the slot along your mat-cutter's guide rail. But that would be a mistake. The slot is there for use with a 90-degree straight cutting head (for sizing) and is not meant to be used with your 45-degree bevel

cutting head (for windows). If you attempt to leave out the underlayment and bevel-cut into the slot, you will soon get ragged cuts, because in punctur-ing the matboard with the blade, you will erupt the face paper into the air space, producing a ragged edge.

CHANGING CUTTER BLADE

The underlayment's ability to provide clean cuts should enable you to go on cutting for some time before a blade change is needed. A ragged cut will signal you when it's time to change the blade, but another sign of a dull blade may reveal itself long before that: when a wavering occurs along the mat's beveled edge. A blade fresh from the pack will slice through the matboard with little resist-ance, but as the blade becomes increasingly dull, it will drag more. The more it drags, the greater its tendency to flex. So another way to avoid wavering bevels is to change the blade whenever blade flex rears its ugly head.

CONQUERING OVERCUTS AND UNDERCUTS

Overcuts, another common mat-cutting problem, occur when the blade passes beyond the corner of the window, leaving a small but noticeable incision in the face of the mat. This is not the fault of the equipment. It happens because of the wide variety of matboard thicknesses, which causes overcuts, as well as undercuts, directly related to the particular thickness of the matboard you are cutting.

All mat cutters are designed so the bevel-cutting blade penetrates the mat at an angle. Because the mat is cut face down, the blade penetrates the back of the mat at a point farther back than it emerges from the face. This is why, whenever you

Overcuts are small incisions that pass beyond the corner of the window into the face of the mat.

cut a mat, there is more overcut in evidence on the back of the mat than on the face. Because the blade is housed in the mat cutter at an angle, if the blade is set too deeply, it also extends out too far, so when you reach the end of the cut, you pass beyond the corner and get an overcut. One way to get rid of an overcut is to adjust your blade depth for the thickness of your matboard, which would be a serviceable solution if all matboard were of the same thickness. But since it is not, if you change to another color or texture of matboard and that next sheet is slightly thicker, you'll get an undercut. If it's thinner, you'll get an overcut.

ADJUSTING INDICATOR LINES

Professional framers typically use some form of compensation to deal with the overcut/undercut problem. Many have mat cutters that allow them to see the penetration point of the blade in relation to the marked lines they have drawn on the back of the mat. If they see overcuts occurring, they simply move the point of penetration in relation to the marked line. Most mat cutters designed for do-it-yourselfers have a start and stop indicator line etched on the cutting head to show the operator where to begin and end each cut in relation to the marked lines. Because different matboard thicknesses affect overcuts and undercuts, the start and stop line on the cutting head cannot possibly be accurate all the time. It's important to realize that the indicator line is only a frame of reference and must be moved backward or forward in relation to the marked line to compensate for overcuts and undercuts. Everyone who gets consistently good results in matting does this.

A workable approach to overcuts is to set your mat cutter to cut borders wider than those determined from your measuring. By doing so, you will be cutting in the mat area that will eventually be the scrap piece that drops from the window. Cutting there allows you to make test cuts in the same piece of matboard from which your window is cut. Make two cuts to form a corner, starting and stopping on the marked lines. Looking at the face of

The start and stop indicator line is only a frame of reference and must be moved back and forth in relation to the marked line to achieve zero overcuts.

A burnishing bone is used to clean up overcuts.

the mat, observe the degree of overcut or undercut. Use this diagnosis to determine the degree by which you will have to move the start and stop indicator line in relation to the marked lines to get a good corner. Then adjust back to the correct border settings and cut your mat.

BURNISHING

But what if you slip and still get an overcut? No problem. Just do what the pros do. Use a tool called a *burnishing bone* to clean up and conceal your overcut. A burnishing bone (sometimes called a *bone folder*) is a narrow burnishing tool reminiscent of a letter opener. It narrows to a tiny, rounded point for the purpose of burnishing over a small area, such as an overcut. When the blade passes beyond the corner into the face of the mat, the paper fibers are pushed up out of the incision like the wake out of the back of a boat. The overcut is pronounced and noticeable because you are looking into this cleft. By burnishing over it, you push the fibers back into the cleft, in effect healing the cut, which is still there, but is less noticeable.

BASIC SINGLE MAT

The basic process of cutting a beveled window in a mat involves three steps: (1) setting the mat guide; (2) marking the mat; and (3) cutting out the window. With a 32" mat cutter or anything larger it's a fairly simple process.

SETTING MAT GUIDE

A mat guide is an adjustable, flat metal bar that lies on the cutting bed in the area immediately adjacent to the guide rail. The guide rail is a second long, flat metal bar that remains fixed in place on the cutting bed and acts as a straightedge for the cutting head to slide against. The mat guide always works in combination with a measuring scale, allowing you to set the mat guide in a precise location indicative of the mat border that you wish to cut. On some systems, it's important that the knobs, which loosen the mat guide and allow it to be moved, are pressed down firmly, after loosening. This releases a safety catch that makes it difficult to move the mat guide, unless it is released.

The mat guide lies parallel to the guide rail and can be slid closer to it or farther away. Setting it closer allows you to mark and cut narrower mat borders; farther away lets you cut wider borders. Consult your measuring notes to recall the mat borders that you determined during the measuring process. Then set the mat guide accordingly on the scale, fixing it in place by tightening the knobs.

Lift the guide rail and place the mat blank, already reduced from the larger sheet, under the guide rail, face down. Place it so that one of its perimeter edges is pressed firmly against the mat guide. Be sure that the correct edge is against the mat guide before going further. If you had decided that all four borders were to be the same, it would not matter, but if you want balanced borders or a weighted border, how you place the mat in the mat cutter will be important.

MARKING THE MAT

Remember that balanced-border mats usually have narrower borders on either side of the window than the ones at the top and bottom. To mark the side borders, place the mat blank under the guide rail with one of its long sides against the mat guide. Mark the mat with a pencil line drawn along the outside edge of the guide rail for the full length of the back of the mat. Keep your pencil tip in as close as possible to the edge of the guide rail as you mark. Spin the mat around 180 degrees and place the opposite long side of the mat against the guide. Mark again, then reset the guide for the remaining pair of borders, and mark those.

To mark out a weighted-border mat, mark the first three borders; then reset the guide and mark the deeper bottom border. For a mat with four equal borders, leave the guide set; spin the mat a quarter turn each time to make a new mark.

CUTTING THE WINDOW

After marking the final line, place the mat back under the guide rail as it was when you made your last mark. Put your bevel cutter against the guide rail. If you have the kind of cutter that clips on the guide rail, make sure to affix it before you attempt to cut; otherwise, all your cuts will be a quarter-inch inside your marks, giving you a smaller window than you anticipated.

Locate the start and stop indicator on your bevel cutter. If your cutter has a push-style head, start with the indicator aligned with the bottom marked line and finish cutting by aligning it with the top marked line. If you have a pull-type cutter, do the opposite; start with the indicator line on the top marked line and pull back until it aligns with the bottom marked line. Apply firm downward pressure on the blade holder as you cut. Easing up will result in the blade penetrating the mat in patches. If that happens, it's best to discard the blank and start over again. Patchy cutting is a common problem for beginners as they try to get a feel for how much pressure is needed to penetrate a mat. The problem is overcome with the experience of cutting just a few mats.

To cut a balanced-border mat, after the first cut, spin the mat 180 degrees and cut the opposite border; then reset the guide to cut the remaining pair of borders. Only if you are cutting all four borders the same do you have the luxury of simply turning the mat a quarter turn after each cut to make the next cut. Recognizing the utility of this,

many professional framers favor mats that have four equal borders. Not surprisingly, such mats have grown in popularity.

After cutting, if your cut is not precisely on the marked line, don't fret. The offset is compensated for in the design of the cutting head. The cut will appear at the exact distance from the perimeter edge that you set the mat guide for.

When you have finished cutting, you have turned your mat blank into a window mat. The dropout piece will fall free, revealing a window with a nice beveled edge.

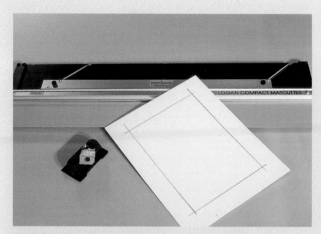

BASIC SINGLE MAT: MARKING. All four lines are marked out in pencil on the back of the mat. The object next to the mat in front of the cutter is the bevel cutting head.

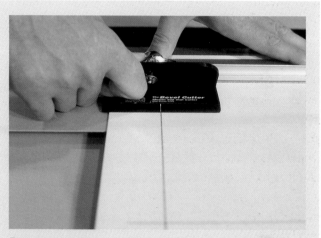

BASIC SINGLE MAT: FIRST CUT. Begin cutting with the start and stop indicator line on the bottom pencil line. Adjust off the pencil line to reduce or eliminate overcuts.

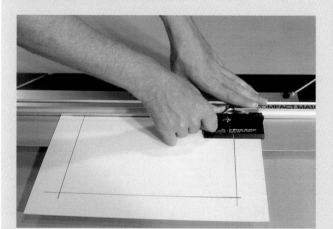

BASIC SINGLE MAT: FINAL CUT. Stop cutting when the start and stop indicator line reaches the top pencil line.

BASIC SINGLE MAT, COMPLETED. The drop-out piece falls cleanly from the window. When the mat is turned over, the window reveals a nice beveled edge.

DOUBLE MAT

A double mat is just two single mats stacked together, in which the window of the top mat, or overmat, is slightly larger than the window of the bottom mat, or undermat. In consequence, the undermat is revealed as a narrow band of color, called the liner, along the window edges of the overmat. The two mats are cut separately, and the double matting process always begins by cutting the overmat in precisely the same manner as that described above for cutting a basic single mat. Nevertheless, the process becomes a bit peculiar as you prepare to cut the undermat.

Before cutting a window in the blank that will be your undermat, put it into your cutter and trim about a ½" from the long side and ½" from the short side. So if your blank is 8 x 10" to begin with, it will now be 7½ x 9½". You don't have to be precise when trimming the edges of the blank. In fact, the undermat doesn't even have to be cut at proper right angles. It can be

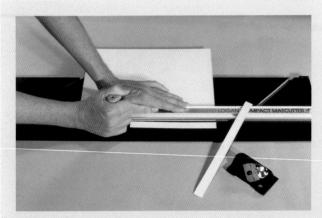

DOUBLE MAT: TRIM. Cut about ½" from the short side and ½" from the long side of your undermat.

DOUBLE MAT: TAPE BORDER. Apply adhesive transfer tape to the back of the window mat in the middle of each border.

DOUBLE MAT: TAPE THE DROPOUT. Replace the dropout piece in the window and apply transfer tape to the back of it.

DOUBLE MAT: JOIN UNDERMAT. Tape the undermat that you trimmed earlier to the back of the window mat. In the example pictures, the undermat is black on its face, which will be revealed as a black liner in the finished double mat.

out of square and will still suffice for your purposes here.

Now comes the odd part. Before cutting a window in the undermat, tape it face down to the back of the overmat, using adhesive transfer tape. Replace the dropout piece in the window of the overmat, then use adhesive transfer tape on the back of the overmat, applying a line of tape within each border and in the middle of the back of the dropout piece. Place the undermat face down on the tape, being careful to position it within the perimeter edges of the overmat.

Adjust the mat guide to ¼" wider than the previous setting, then mark out the undermat and cut it while it is taped to the overmat. A double dropout piece will fall from the window, revealing a perfectly aligned double mat. The secret of perfect alignment is found not only in the fact that the undermat is smaller than the overmat, but also because the perimeter edges of the overmat are the only edges used to align the mat during the cutting process. By taping the undermat within the perimeter edges of the overmat, you use the perimeter edges of the overmat to measure, mark, align, and cut the window in the undermat. As a result, the two mats come out perfectly aligned.

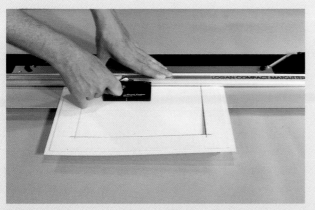

DOUBLE MAT: CUT UNDERMAT. With the undermat taped face down on the back of the overmat, cut it, using the same method as that employed for a single mat.

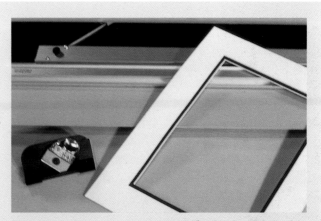

DOUBLE MAT, COMPLETED. A perfectly aligned double mat is created. Note that the undermat is revealed as a black liner along the window edges of the overmat.

MARY RUSSELL
Empress

Note how all of the framing choices are coordinated with the palette and spirit of the artwork in this alternate example of a strong mat design.

MULTIPLE-OPENING MAT

utting a mat that has more than one window is a common technique that is often used for framing a series of photographs, each with its own opening within a mat. If you are a novice framer, you may only foresee the need for single mat windows and brush aside the need to learn multiple openings. However, as soon as bargain-hunting friends and relatives discover your ability to mat, they may come to you for help, since multiple-opening mats are greatly in demand but are very costly when custom-made by a frame shop.

Multiple-opening mats in which the windows are all the same size and orientation can be managed by a neophyte. But multiple openings with various sizes and orientations of windows can be a measuring and designing nightmare. So take things one step at a time. At this stage, keep all your windows the same size to simplify matters.

Begin by noting the sizes of the items you want to mat. Typically, if you have photos of various sizes, select the smallest ones and figure your windows to accommodate those. Larger pictures can still be displayed, but a portion of the image will have to be sacrificed when you position it in the window, which will be slightly smaller than the photo. So if the photos are 4 x 6", the windows should be 3¾ x 5¾", allowing the windows to overlap the photos and help hold them in place.

CALCULATING INDIVIDUAL WINDOW SIZE

After determining the number of windows your mat will need, calculate the total measure of the windows by rows. First, add together the widths of all the windows in a single row. For example, if you want to cut a mat with six windows in two rows of three each, with all the windows oriented vertically, each window being 3¾" wide, the horizontal sum of all the windows in that row would then be 11¼" (3¾" x 3 = 11¼").

Now do the same for the height of all the windows in a single column. Two rows of three across gives you two windows in each vertical column; each is 5¾" high, making the total height of windows in a column 11½" (5¾ x 2 = 11½"). The purpose of this is to determine how much space the windows take up if combined into a single window.

In other words, six windows of 3¾ x 5 ¾" take up the same amount of space as a single window of 11¼ x 11½".

CALCULATING BRACKETING BORDERS

The next step is establishing the correct mat borders—called the bracketing borders—that surround the windows. They should be 1¾". This measurement is found by consulting the "Border Finder" (page 21). In the example cited, the combined window size is 11¼ x 11½"; added together, that equals 22¾" united inches, which falls between 12" and 24" on the "Border Finder," directing us to starting borders of 1¾" for the bracketing borders of the multiple-opening mat. Then, to decide how much space will go between each window, we are guided by a basic rule of thumb: The spaces between each window can be no wider than the bracketing borders, but they can be narrower. To ascertain how wide they should be, we must experiment, adding the spaces, windows, and bracketing borders, to arrive at a frame size. Since we will want our frame size to be in full inches, with no fractions, we will probably have to tweak the spaces between the windows.

For example, three windows of 3¾", with bracketing borders of 1¾", take up 13" of space. If the spaces between the windows are the same width as the bracketing borders, 1¾", it brings us to a total frame width of 16½", which is no good because it has a fraction in it. However, if we make the spaces between the windows 1½", we get a

MULTIPLE-OPENING MAT: MEASURE, MARK. After reducing your full-size sheet to your frame size, mark out the windows on the back of the mat. This is most easily accomplished if you have a 40½" mat cutter with a squaring arm. Use its mat guide to mark out the bracketing borders and use the ruler on the squaring arm to mark out the spaces between the windows.

MULTIPLE-OPENING MAT: POSITIONING CUTTER. The body of the cutting head must pass through the window area as defined by the marked lines. If the body of the cutting head passes outside the lines, you will create a reverse bevel. That means the beveled edges will appear on the back of the mat, not the front, which cannot be corrected; the mat will be ruined.

MULTIPLE-OPENING MAT: USING GUIDE RAIL. Use the guide rail as a straightedge, placing its edge along the marked lines. As you turn the mat to cut it, large portions of the mat will extend to the left of the guide rail where the mat guide would normally be. Before cutting, remove the mat guide; it will be in the way when cutting a multiple-opening mat.

MULTIPLE-OPENING MAT: CONTINUE FOLLOWING PENCIL LINES. Start and stop on the pencil lines that define the window you are cutting out.

frame width of 16", which is just fine. Therefore, on the width dimension, we will make the spaces between the windows 1½", marginally narrower than the bracketing borders.

For the height dimension, we have two windows of 5¾", with bracketing borders of 1¾". With space between the windows of 1½", we get a total frame height of 16½", which is no good. To rectify the problem, we could make the space between the windows 2", but then spaces between all six windows would not be uniform; it would look as if the windows were floating apart. Instead, we can make all the spaces on both dimensions uniform, with the top and bottom bracketing borders slightly wider than the bracketing side borders, creating a balanced-border look. To summarize: The top and bottom bracketing borders are 2½", which, when combined with two windows of 5¾" and a space of 1½" would yield a frame height of 16"—which works out fine.

As you can see, much of the work in creating a multiple opening is in measuring. Once you've conquered that, it's relatively smooth sailing. Referring to the photos and captions that follow:

Once you've had a few successful experiences with mats in which all the windows are the same size, you might want to attempt one with different sizes and configurations. Trace out the windows on a sheet of paper, cut them out, and stick them to a matboard. Once you're satisfied as to the layout, mark around the cutouts and proceed to cut the mat.

If you find the multiple-opening a challenge, the next level is even more demanding, albeit no less popular: the double multiple-opening mat.

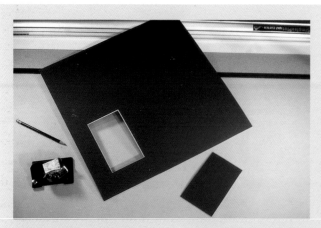

MULTIPLE-OPENING MAT: FIRST WINDOW CUT. Here we see the front of the mat with the first window cut out. Concentrate on one window at a time. Cut each completely before moving on to the next. This will help you remain focused and avoid reverse bevels.

MULTIPLE-OPENING MAT, COMPLETED. The finished multiple-window mat has a number of uses. In addition to framing photographs, think of assembling miniature pieces of art, foreign paper currency brought home from a trip, or other mementos for framed display.

M. DAVID LOGAN
Friends and Family
The tone of the wood frame and its gold accent give treasured photos a distinguished setting for permanent display.

DOUBLE MULTIPLE-OPENING MAT

Alignment is the problem with the double multiple-opening mat. Getting the two mats to line up so that the band of color from the undermat is uniform in each window is not easily accomplished by either of the usual methods. If you cut the overmat and undermat separately and try to tape them together, it won't work. If you cut the top mat first, and then tape the two mats together before cutting the undermat, the preferred method for a standard double mat as detailed above, that won't work either. You will find the windows get progressively out of alignment with each succeeding window in a row.

The correct method is a bit more complicated. Cut your mat blanks to size, then stack them together, using tape to adhere them temporarily along their perimeter edges. Measure and mark out the openings in pencil on the back of the undermat. When doing that, think in terms of the fin-

ished mat, the one that will consist of the overmat and a band of color from the undermat, an exposure of about ¼" along each edge. When marking the undermat, then, mark the actual opening. The opening of the overmat, which you will mark later, will have to be ¼" larger on each edge to expose the band of the color from the undermat.

One of the difficulties in measuring and marking a double multiple-opening mat is in keeping straight what is the "undermat" and what is the "overmat." You must always think of the two mats in terms of how they will appear in the final presentation. So, even though you have flipped the two mats over and are working with them face down, the overmat, which is now the undermat, is still the one on top, and the undermat is always the one under it, regardless of how you flip it around to work on it. Now, referring to the photos and captions that follow:

DOUBLE MULTIPLE-OPENING MAT: PUNCTURE UNDERMAT. Use a thumbtack to puncture the undermat at the corners of the marked-out window openings.

DOUBLE MULTIPLE-OPENING MAT: HINGE. You are now looking down at the back of the overmat. You will find it riddled with puncture marks which, if connected by lines, would reveal the exact position of each window. Apply adhesive transfer tape within each window area as defined by the puncture marks. Then hinge the undermat back down so the two mats stick together.

DOUBLE MULTIPLE-OPENING MAT: CUT. Put the mats in your cutter and cut the windows in the undermat. Remember, as with any multiple-opening mat, it's important to watch where you're cutting. The cutting head should travel through the defined area of each window, lest a reverse bevel result and your mat be ruined.

DOUBLE MULTIPLE-OPENING MAT: MEASURE. With the cut undermat lifted off to the side, what remains is the overmat with the fallout pieces of the undermat stuck to it. These fallout pieces are important because they will be your guide in marking out the overmat. Using a ruler, measure out from the edges of the fallout pieces ¼" and make guide marks.

DOUBLE MULTIPLE-OPENING MAT: CUT. With the dropout pieces pulled away from the overmat and any remaining adhesive removed by rubbing over it with your thumb, lay the straightedge along the guide marks and mark out the openings on the back of the top mat. Then cut the openings in the overmat.

DOUBLE MULTIPLE-OPENING MAT: APPLY ADHESIVE. After cutting, apply adhesive transfer tape to the back of the overmat.

DOUBLE MULTIPLE-OPENING MAT: JOIN. Position the overmat carefully on top of the undermat and adhere the two together.

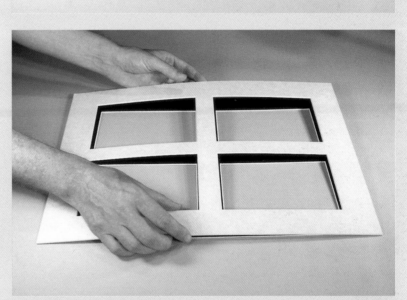

DOUBLE MULTIPLE-OPENING MAT, COMPLETED. The double multiple-opening mat is now completed, with its band of color from the undermat (the liner) uniformly aligned in all four windows.

As its name implies, this style of mat has an alcove cut into its bottom border to reveal a title. Like the previous project, creating this mat requires much in terms of measuring, but is surprisingly easy to cut.

Begin by measuring the artwork or other material to be framed, paying particular attention to the area of the title and the margin of white space surrounding it that you want to reveal. For example, if you have an image that measures 24 x 30" and a title below it that is 4½" long with letters ⅝" high, if you want to reveal ½" of white space surrounding the title, you will need an indent of 5½" x 1⅝".

To determine your frame size, add your borders to your window size. For example, to expose ½" of white space around the image, the window size will be 25 x 31". For borders of 3½", your frame will be 32 x 38". Subtract the width of your proposed title indent from the width of your frame size to discover what you have available to work with in terms of side borders for your title indent. Thus, by subtracting 5½" from 32", you have 26½" to work with. Dividing that number in half to find the width of borders on either side of your title indent, half of 26½" yields borders of 13¼" on either side of the indent.

To find the bottom border of your title indent, subtract the height of the proposed indent from the height of the bottom border: that is, 1⅝" from 3½" gives you 1⅜".

With measuring completed, we turn to marking out the mat and subsequent steps, per the photos and captions that follow:

TITLE INDENT MAT: MEASURE, MARK. On the back of a mat of 32 x 38", mark borders of 3½" for the presentation window; 13¼" as the width borders of your title indent; 1⅜" for the bottom border of your title indent.

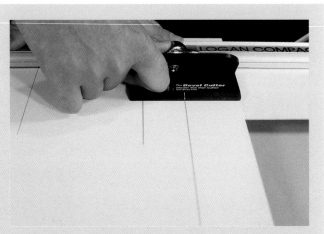

TITLE INDENT MAT: BEGIN WINDOW CUT. With the mat guide set, cut the three sides of the presentation window that are not bisected by a line defining the title indent.

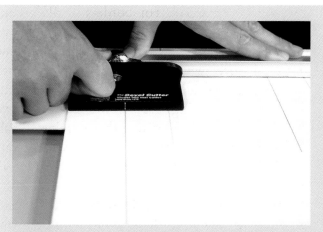

TITLE INDENT MAT: FINISH WINDOW CUT. With the mat turned so lines defining the title indent are on the left, align your guide rail along the remaining border of your presentation window and cut.

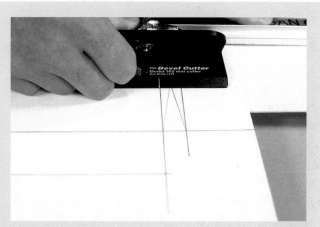

TITLE INDENT MAT: CUT INDENT. With the mat guide removed, align the guide rail along a line that defines one of the side borders of the title indent. Cut between a point roughly in the middle of the dropout piece and the line that defines the bottom of the title indent.

TITLE INDENT MAT: CUT INDENT BORDERS. With the guide rail aligned along the line that defines the bottom border of the title indent, cut, starting and stopping on the lines that define the right and left borders of the title indent.

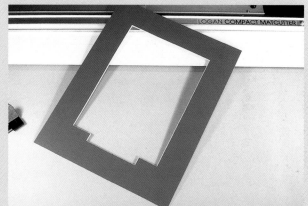

TITLE INDENT MAT, COMPLETED. With the guide rail set along the line that defines the left border of the title indent, the final cut is made between the line that defines the bottom of the title indent and a point roughly in the middle of the dropout piece. When that piece falls away, the title indent mat is complete.

TITLE WINDOW MAT

Of all matting techniques, the title window is perhaps the most deceptive. On the surface, it's a simple matter of cutting a narrow aperture beneath the larger window in the face of the mat, but locating that little window can be tricky, and because every title-to-image orientation is different, the process is difficult to comprehend in principle. So it's better to focus on a single example.

Begin by measuring the area of the title. Allow at least ¼" of blank space around each side, which will give you the actual size of the title window. For example, measuring the letters (including spaces between words) in your title, from far left to far right, your title would be roughly 5½" wide; adding ¼" to either side, your title window would be 6" across. Letters ¾" in height would call for a title window 1¼" high.

To figure the measurements of the larger window and the mat borders surrounding it, if you have a horizontally oriented image of 12½ x 10" and want to show ¼" of blank space around it, the window will be 13 x 10½".

Mat borders of 2" on the sides and top will be adequate, but with a title window the bottom border should be wider by at least the height of the title window. Here, that would be at least 3¼". However, if you add a 3¼" border to a 10½" window height with a 2" top border, you'll end up with an overall frame height of 15¾". Since it's preferable to have a standard, full-inch frame height, adjust the measure to 16" with an additional ¼" on the bottom border, making it 3½".

Now the title window must be centered in the bottom border. The height of the bottom border is 3½"; the width is the same as the frame width, in our example, 17" wide. So your challenge is to position a title window of 6 x 1¼" into a bottom border of 17 x 3½".

Determine the borders flanking the title window by subtracting the width of the title window, 6", from the width of the mat, 17", giving you

11"; divide that in half, and your side borders are 5½" for the title window.

Next, find the distance between the bottom edge of the title window and the perimeter edge of the mat, and at the same time, between the top edge of the title window and the bottom edge of the larger window. This is a bit more complicated.

It won't do just to center the title window top to bottom in the border; you must take into account the distance between the bottom of the image and the title. The title may be closer to the image or farther away. So you must measure the distance from the bottom of the image to the middle of the characters in the title. In our example, that distance is 1½".

The blank space between the bottom of the image and the bottom edge of the window must be considered next. Earlier, it was decided to show a ¼" of blank space around the image, so there is ¼" between the bottom of the image and the bottom edge of the window. To position the title window, find its midpoint. Subtract the blank space between the bottom of the image and the bottom of the window from the space between the bottom of the image and the middle of the characters that form the title. In our example, the difference is 1¼" (1½" minus ¼" equals 1¼"). Therefore, 1¼" is the distance between the middle of the title and the bottom edge of the larger window.

Next, to find the distance between the top edge of the title window and the bottom edge of the larger window, divide in half the height of the title window and subtract the result from the distance between the middle of the title and the bottom edge of the larger window. In our example, the height of the title window is 1¼"; half of that is ⅝". Subtracting ⅝" from 1¼", we get ⅝". This is the distance from the top edge of the title window to the bottom edge of the larger window; ⅝" applies to the next step as well.

For the distance from the title window's bottom edge and the edge of the mat, add the ⅝" to the height of the title window (1¼") and subtract the sum from the height of the bottom border (3½"). The answer is 1⅝".

Summarizing the example, here's how the bottom border will look: Distance from the edge of the mat to bottom of the title window is 1⅝"; height of the title window, 1¼"; distance from the top of the title window to the bottom edge of the larger window, ⅝"; height of bottom border, 3½"; width of title window, 6"; side borders to title window, 5½". Using the measurements determined above, proceed to cut your mat by referring to the eight photos and instructional captions that follow.

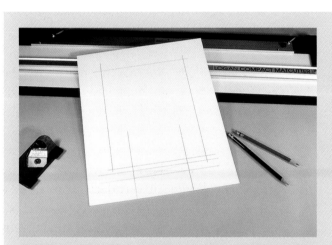

TITLE WINDOW MAT: MARK. After all measures have been marked, place an X inside the title window area so you can more easily identify it when cutting. Note that the mat guide has been removed; it should be kept off during cutting.

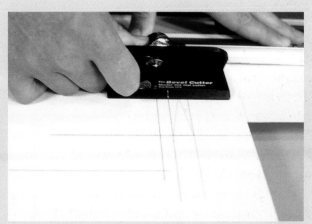

TITLE WINDOW MAT: FIRST CUT. Cut the title window first. Begin by working on the short sides.

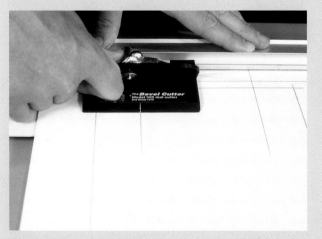

TITLE WINDOW MAT: SECOND CUT. Cut the bottom of the title window. Remember that the cutting head must travel through the area you are cutting out.

TITLE WINDOW MAT: THIRD CUT. To cut the top of the title window, tape a second piece of matboard adjacent to the mat and extend the pencil lines out onto it so you'll know where to start and stop.

TITLE WINDOW MAT: FOURTH CUT. Stop and start on the lines extended out to the supplementary matboard.

TITLE WINDOW MAT: FIFTH CUT. Cut the title window out completely.

TITLE WINDOW MAT: SIXTH CUT. Now that the title window is cut, work on the larger opening, starting and stopping on the lines that define the presentation window.

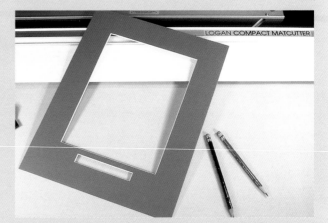

TITLE WINDOW MAT, COMPLETED. The finished mat has a simple appearance, but looks can be deceiving. Measuring complexities and cutting challenges make this mat one of the more difficult ones to master.

STEPPED-CORNER MAT

Overflowing with style, the stepped-corner mat, also called the offset corner mat, is distinctive and versatile. It can be created with any number of right-angled steps in each corner, in various size combinations.

Begin by determining the size of the window you're going to cut. Our example has a window of 15½ x 19½" in a frame of 20 x 24", requiring mat borders of 2¼". Reduce a full-size matboard sheet to the frame size. Referring to the eight photos and instructional captions below, proceed to mark and cut your mat as follows:

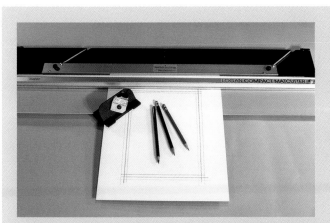

STEPPED-CORNER MAT: MARK. Using red, black, and blue pencils on the back of your mat, mark out three rectangles, each inside the next, each ¼" apart. Rule the black 2¾" border first; inside that, the blue, ¼" away, at 2½"; the third, in red, ¼" away, at 2¼".

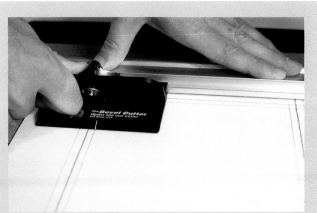

STEPPED-CORNER MAT: START CUT, OUTERMOST RECTANGLE. Position your mat by aligning the outermost rectangle, the red, along the guide rail, then begin your cut with the start/stop indicator line on the *innermost* rectangle, the black one.

STEPPED-CORNER MAT: END CUT, OUTERMOST RECTANGLE. Cut to the line that defines the top of the innermost rectangle, again, the black one. Cut all four sides of the outermost rectangle, starting and stopping on the lines marked in black ink. When you have finished, you will find that the cuts have not met in the corners. That is correct.

STEPPED-CORNER MAT: START CUT, MIDDLE RECTANGLE. Adjust your mat guide to 2½" and position your mat by aligning the middle rectangle, the blue, along the guide rail. Begin your cut with the start/stop indicator on the middle rectangle, the blue one.

STEPPED-CORNER MAT: END CUT, MIDDLE RECTAN-GLE. To finish cutting the middle rectangle, stop on the blue line. During this set of cuts, starts/stops are on the rectangle you are cutting, so the dropout piece will fall from the window.

STEPPED-CORNER MAT: START CUT, INNERMOST REC-TANGLE. Adjust your mat guide to 2¾" and position your mat by aligning the innermost rectangle, the black, along the guide rail. Begin your cut with the start/stop indicator on the outermost rectangle, the red one.

STEPPED-CORNER MAT: END CUT, INNERMOST REC-TANGLE. Finish cutting all four sides of the innermost rectangle, starting and stopping on the red lines. During this set of cuts, you must keep the dropout piece in the window so the cutting head can remain level while you work. As you cut, slim strips of matboard will fall out. Brush them away, but leave the dropout piece in place. If it shifts during cutting, that's okay, but you must keep it in during this step.

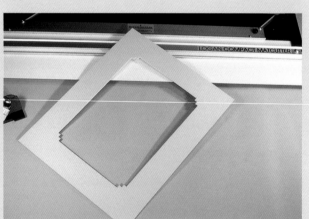

STEPPED-CORNER MAT, COMPLETED. The finished mat, as seen with its face side up, has two steps in each corner, evoking a delightful art deco effect.

EIGHT-SIDED WINDOW MAT

High-end mat-cutting equipment often includes an impressive accessory known as an *angle plate,* which marks out and holds a mat blank for cutting a window with oblique angles (as opposed to right angles). But that tool is not the only option for cutting eight-sided mats, diamond-shaped windows, and others with oblique angles.

If you own a mat cutter that has a guide rail, indeed you can cut oblique-angled mats, and for a lot less than the cost of an angle plate. All you need is a 45-degree, plastic triangle (the kind children use in geometry class—should cost less than a dollar) to cut an impressive angled mat like the one shown in the six photos with instructional captions that follow:

EIGHT-SIDED WINDOW: MARK. Set your mat guide and mark out borders of 1¾"; reset your mat guide to 3½", insert the mat, and mark again. Each corner has a marked-out square. Mark lines from corner to corner of each square, defining the angles. Remove the mat guide.

EIGHT-SIDED WINDOW: CUT CORNERS. Cut your corner angles first. Preparing to do that, align one corner along the guide rail, keeping most of the mat to the right of the rail. Using a 45-degree triangle, place its long edge against the guide rail, and the corner of the triangle at the corner of the marked square. Draw a pencil line along the full length of the bottom of the triangle. Repeat this with the other corner of the square. You have now provided yourself with pencil lines to start/stop on when you cut your angled corners.

EIGHT-SIDED WINDOW: REINFORCE LINES. Set the mat guide for 1¾" and insert the mat. To help you visualize, use a red pencil to mark over the straight lines that connect the angled cuts.

EIGHT-SIDED WINDOW: CUT STRAIGHT LINES. As you cut, start and stop each cut on the lines that extend out from the bottom of each corner square.

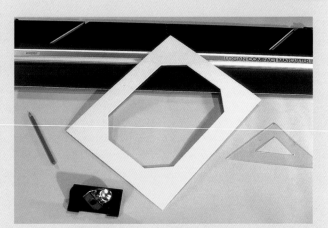

EIGHT-SIDED WINDOW: CONNECT CUTS. After each cut, you will see that you are connecting the angled cuts with straight cuts.

EIGHT-SIDED WINDOW, COMPLETED. When you are finished, a decorative eight-sided mat is the result.

OVAL OR ROUND MAT

Reliable oval and round mat cutting used to be reserved for professional framers. Even today, a range of expensive cutters can create a remarkable variety of sizes, from dime-shaped circles to ovals as large as a wading pool. But, as described in the chapter dealing with equipment (see page 64), the Logan 3-Step Oval and Circle Mat Cutter, a hand tool, does just as good a job at a fraction of the cost, producing ovals from 3½ x 4" to 20 x 23" and circles in a similar range.

The 3-Step does requires practice in learning how to operate it to best effect, without making mistakes. If you take time to learn the ropes, the rewards are many. Here are some insights to help you get good results faster. Just follow these seven photos and instructional captions:

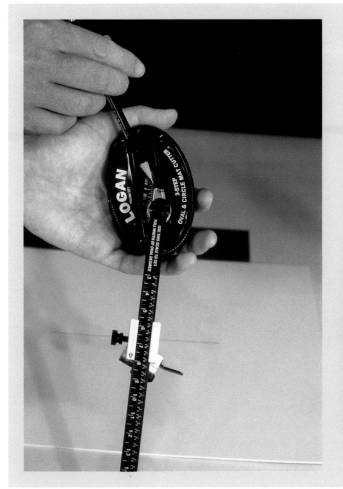

OVAL/ROUND MATS: SET SCALE. A bevel-cutting head mounted to an arm rotates around a stationary base. A cam-shaped plate with a sliding midpoint allows for the setting of different ellipses, each shape adjusted by setting the scale inside the base. By locating the midpoint at dead center, you can cut circles.

OVAL/ROUND MATS: MARK. To position the oval cutter on the mat, mark the face of your mat with a large plus sign (larger than the base) where you want the middle of the oval to be. Place another mat underneath to prevent cutting into your tabletop.

OVAL/ROUND MATS: POSITION BASE. Line up the white marks on the sides of the base with the arms of the plus sign you've marked. All cutting is done on the face of the mat.

OVAL/ROUND MATS: ANCHOR BASE. Using the heels of your hands, press down on the base. Pins underneath the base anchor the base to the mat, but you must still hold down firmly on the base at all times as you cut.

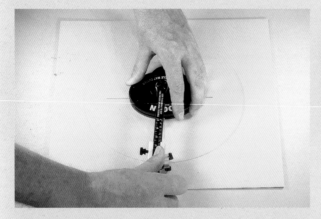

OVAL/ROUND MATS: READY TO CUT. With your non-cutting hand, press firmly on the base. Then grasp the rotating arm with your thumb resting lightly atop the cutting head. Make one full rotation of the arm around the base with the blade disengaged, so that the cutting head may track into the proper position before cutting.

OVAL/ROUND MATS: CUT. With your thumb resting lightly on top of the cutting head, reach down with your index finger and lift the stepping lever to the first step, to lower the blade. Begin cutting. There are three cutting rotations. The blade is lowered a step after each rotation.

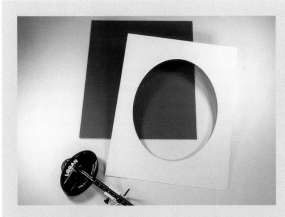

OVAL/ROUND MATS, COMPLETED. After three rotations of the cutting head, the dropout piece will fall, revealing your oval window. Circular windows are made in the same way with a simple adjustment of the cutter. The Logan 3-Step Oval and Circle Mat Cutter creates a neat 45-degree bevel.

SALLY ALATALO (RIGHT)
Sally As Mother

An oval mat is an especially appropriate choice with portraiture, lending a traditional look associated with studio photography of an earlier age.

INSIDER TIPS FOR SUCCESSFUL OVAL/ROUND WINDOWS

With mats 16 x 20" or less, keep your cutting hand in position on the arm as you turn the *base* counterclockwise with your other hand, spinning the mat and backing sheet into position, then sweeping the arm down to make the cut.

With larger mats, keep the mat and backing sheet stationary, and exchange the position of your hands on the arm and the base, after each sweep of the arm.

Remember, the first cutting rotation is the most critical one; it lightly scores the surface of the mat. As you grasp the arm, be sure your fingers are well out of the way of the cutting head; it swivels, and if your fingers creep down and contact it, you will restrict its ability to turn, knocking it out of alignment and fraying the bevel.

The cutting head only cuts if you rotate the arm around the base in a clockwise direction. If you attempt to turn the arm counterclockwise, you will knock the head out of alignment and fray the bevel.

If, after lifting away the base, you find that you have not fully penetrated the mat, retract the blade and carefully realign the base pins with the holes they have made in the mat. Rotate the arm once around the base without cutting, to get the head into proper alignment again, then lift the stepping lever to the first step. Make about a quarter of a rotation; then look closely to see if the blade is cutting in its original score. If it is, step the blade down to the final setting and continue cutting, exerting additional downward pressure to ensure penetration.

V-GROOVE MAT

arving a groove in the surface of a mat is often viewed as the most elegant way to accent art. Much of this good regard has to do with the perceived difficulty in making the cut, and indeed, in early years, the V-shaped groove was actually carved in the surface of the mat by a fastidious artisan. But now, there are a few ways to cut a V-groove with relative ease.

One method is cutting a reverse bevel on the edge of the dropout piece and replacing it in the window—that is, not cutting a groove in the surface of the mat at all, but cutting two separate pieces with the bevels facing each other, then taping them together on the back. One drawback to this method is that it requires a costly, heavy-duty mat-cutting system that bevel cuts on the left side of the guide rail. For do-it-yourselfers or fledgling pros, its hefty price for the little extra it delivers is unwarranted, and at the end of the day, it doesn't deliver a "real" V-groove. For purists, actually carving a groove in the mat surface remains the ideal.

Early machines for cutting surface V-grooves were flawed because they did not allow for mitered corners, causing grooves that were overcut or that came up short, leaving tufts of paper. But a device recently introduced by Logan Graphic Products has overcome this problem, offering a cutter that is capable of making a perfect V-groove in the surface of a mat without overcuts or undercuts. This V-groove device is compatible with many mat-cutting systems.

With the Logan cutter, to insure perfect mitered corners without overcuts, the blade that cuts the outside edge of the groove cuts marginally farther than the one that cuts the inside edge. Consequently, the cutting head has to be fine-tuned before you start. Delicate adjustments are made to an eccentric post attached to the cutting head that contacts the top stop, and equally delicate adjustments are made to a screw seated in the rear guide that contacts the bottom stop. A piece of scrap matboard should be used to make practice cuts while adjusting.

In addition to overcut/undercut adjustments, the Logan V-Groover allows for adjustment to the width of the V-groove, although making it too wide can result in a torn and gritty V-groove. In fact, a gritty V-groove is the most common prob-

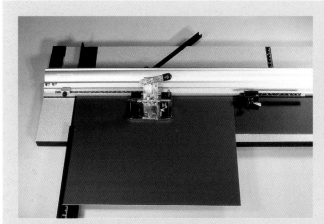

V-GROOVE MAT: ADAPTABILITY. Made by Logan Graphic Products, this device is capable of cutting a perfect V-groove in the surface of a mat. It is compatible with many affordable mat-cutting systems. Here, it is used with a 40½" mat cutter.

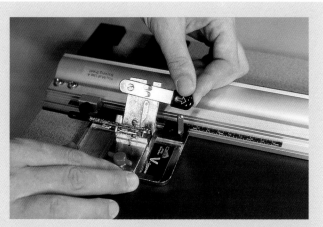

V-GROOVE MAT: LEFT BLADE. Two retractable blades are at opposing 45-degree angles. The blade on the left is lowered by means of a lever, and the cutting head is pushed away from the operator until it contacts a stop. It cuts a 45-degree bevel about halfway into the core of the matboard.

lem with this cutter. It results most often from dull blades, caused by the operator failing to retract one blade before lowering the other. This allows the cutting edges to scrape against each other. Setting the cutting head down while one of the blades is still extended may also dull blades.

These learn-as-you-go problems are due to the sensitivity of the cutter and are to be anticipated with a product having such tight tolerances and requiring such minute adjustments. Thus, taking the time to read the product's instructions is not only advised, but is essential, and doing so will save you a lot of time and headaches. But once you understand and adjust the product properly, you will enjoy consistent, top-quality surface V-grooves, and be able to produce this most elegant and impressive of accents whenever the situation calls for it.

Referring to the photos and instructional captions beginning on page 110, here are the basic steps to follow:

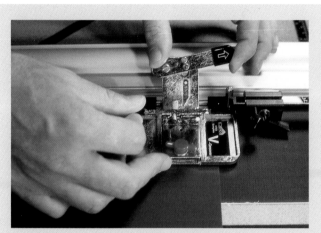

V-GROOVE MAT: RIGHT BLADE. After the blade has contacted the top stop, the blade on the left side is retracted and the blade on the right side is lowered.

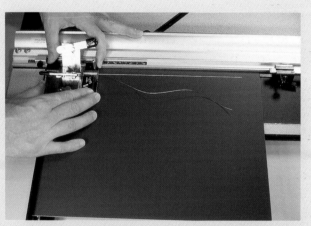

V-GROOVE MAT: LONG CUT. The cutting head is then pulled back until it contacts the bottom stop, cutting an opposing 45-degree bevel about halfway into the core and producing a long, narrow wedge that is easily peeled out to reveal the V-groove.

SARAH BACCI
Brother

Black-and-white photograph: The V-groove mat contributes an elegant and impressive accent to a frame job. Here, its design in black and white coordinates perfectly with the image it surrounds.

V-GROOVE MAT, COMPLETED. The white V-groove in the brown mat surface echos the white beveled edge of the mat window, producing a handsome double-border effect.

FACE PAINTING: DECORATIVE ACCENTS
TURN A MAT INTO ART

Decorative accents can turn mats into works of art unto themselves. With the exception of V-grooves, these accents always entail painting on the face of the mat. The most venerable of this type is the French mat, probably the earliest form of decorative matting.

Strict in its layout, a proper French mat has one painted panel and a total of five inked lines, including those bordering the panel. Watercolor paint is applied in the area between the second and third inked lines. French matting sometimes substitutes acrylic paints or pastel powders, but the watercolor wash is surely the most classical.

Inking lines on the face of a mat can be problematic, whether you are creating a French mat or something as straightforward as a single line scribed around the window. The obvious approach to scribing—simply lining up a straightedge and putting pen to paper—often results in an unsightly blotch where the pen first contacts the mat, and where it ends. Here's a better way:

To place your lines at 1 ½", for example, measure down from the top of the matboard 1 ½" and in from the left edge 1 ½"; make a small tick mark there in pencil, on the face of the mat. Then measure up from the bottom edge and in from the left edge 1 ½" and make another tick mark.

Tear off a small strip of 3M Magic® Tape and place it just above the top tick mark. Place the tape as close as possible to the tick mark. Tear off a second piece of tape and place it just below the bottom tick mark. Place the tape as close as possible to the tick mark.

Line up the straightedge with the tick marks; with a pen, draw a line on the tape. If there is any blotching, it will occur on the tape and when the pen contacts the matboard it will already be moving forward. Mark along the straightedge, keeping the pen moving at a consistent speed. End your mark on the bottom piece of tape. Any blotching that might occur will be on the tape. The purpose of using this particular tape is that it's removable. When you take it off, you'll find that your lines are joined cleanly at the corners.

Decorative accents can become quite elaborate, expanding beyond inked lines into full-blown, painterly effects from marbleing to feathering, and can reach the point where the mat becomes a painting in its own right. At that point, we pass the baton to the artist and retreat to the more familiar footing of traditional picture framing.

After attaching a strip of tape just above the tick mark, start drawing your ink line on the tape, using the tip of your pen.

Mark along the straightedge, keeping the pen moving at a constant speed. Finish marking with the tip of the pen on the tape below the bottom tick mark.

When you peel up the tape, you will find that your ink lines are cleanly joined at the corners.

MARY RUSSELL
Untitled

A French mat with a watercolor wash is among the most venerable and challenging of decorative matting techniques.

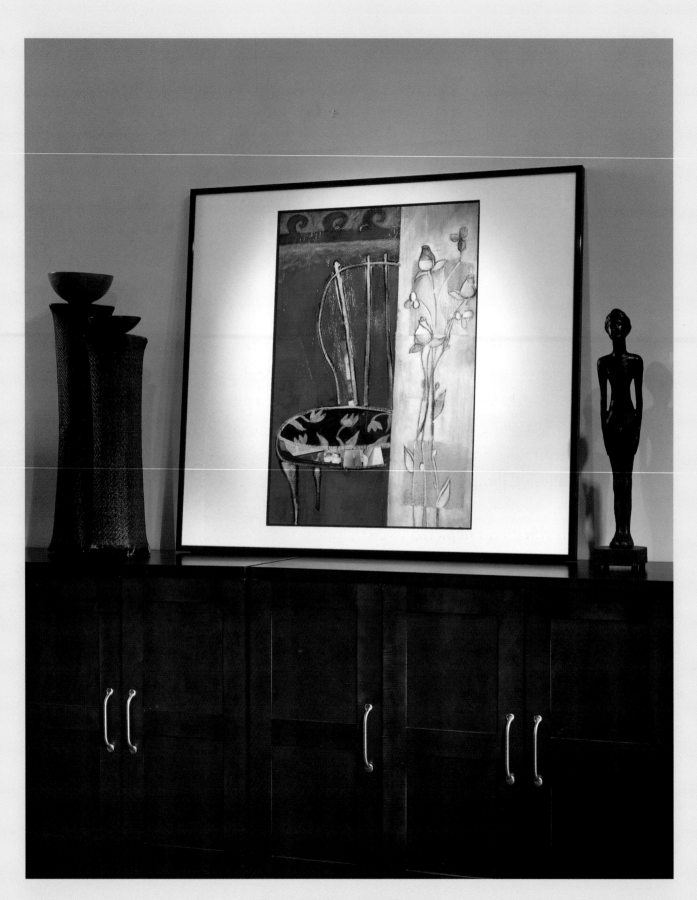

TREY, DELJOU ART GROUP
Art framed with Nielsen molding and Bainbridge Artcare matboards.
Photo compliments of NielsenBainbridge.

STEP 6

MOUNTING

The word *mounting* refers to the method used to secure artwork for presentation, by gluing it, taping it, trapping it, screwing it, or nailing it. Techniques include spray mounting, dry mounting, cold mounting, three types of hinge mounting, nonadhesive mounting, and specialized ways to mount oil paintings, pastels, needlework, and three-dimensional objects. All of these will be described and depicted in detail.

The method you use depends on the type of artwork you are mounting and what you hope to accomplish in terms of conservation. Since conservation is a subject unto itself, and one that causes much consternation in the world of picture framing, let us discuss that before we explore the various ways to mount art.

At its most basic, conservation framing is an effort to ensure that artwork can be taken out of a frame at some future date and be found in the same condition it had been in the day it was mounted. Because the effort to conserve something has the effect of archiving it, many people refer to conservation framing as *archival framing*.

CONSERVATION FRAMING

For the most part, the terms *archival* and *conservation* are interchangeable. But it doesn't end there. The term *acid-free* is used to imply conservation and archival, while *pH neutral, acid-neutralized, buffered,* and *pH balanced* are spun to mean the same thing as acid-free. Throw into the mix *lignin-free* and *museum quality* and you've got a stew that would befuddle the mind of the most earnest conservator. Should you really worry about acid and all those other overlapping and cautionary terms? For starters, let us find out just what those threats are.

ACID: HOW IT THREATENS ARTWORK

Acid is present in lignin, a natural binding polymer that holds wood together. Direct sunlight, high humidity, and time cause the breakdown of lignin. When that happens, acid can seep out of wood, or a wood-based product such as paper, and create a brown haze called *acid burn,* a permanent stain that cannot be removed. If the contaminated item is a valued piece of artwork, it can be a terrible loss.

Therefore, much of what is done in typical conservation framing is to safeguard artwork against acid contamination by using acid-free matboard and other acid-free components that come in contact with the framed artwork.

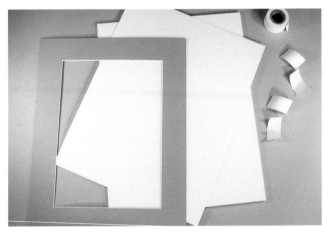

Boards and tapes used in a conservation frame job are acid-free, often made of cotton, rather than wood, to safeguard artwork against acid contamination.

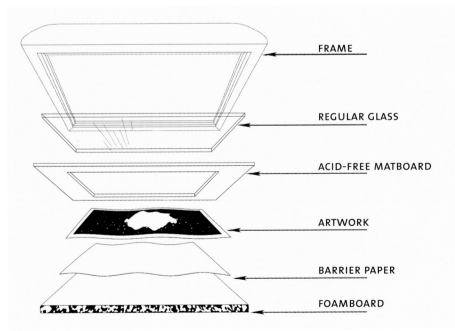

FRAME

REGULAR GLASS

ACID-FREE MATBOARD

ARTWORK

BARRIER PAPER

FOAMBOARD

CONSERVATION FRAMING

All components of a typical conservation frame job are acid-free and lignin-free, except for foamboard, which may have minimal acid content.

MUSEUM FRAMING

Since museums require the highest degree of protection to safeguard their priceless artwork over centuries to come, they go a step further in framing art. A higher grade of cotton matboard is used; mounting tapes are made of lignin-free paper adhered with wheat starch; and glazing is UV-protective glass. But even all of that may not be

The boards and tapes used in a typical museum frame job provide maximum protection for artwork. The little bottle contains pure rice starch adhesive.

enough. What is the frame made of? Museum framers usually seal the frame rabbet to create a barrier against lignin in the wood, but given enough time, acid can work through the barrier and threaten artwork. Putting the components in a metal frame may not solve the problem either; the museum wall may be made of wood, and even if it isn't, acid floating freely in the air can affect artwork over time.

So what is a museum to do? In a word: reframe. In fact, museums take frames apart and start over again on a regular basis. If acid has gotten a foothold in any of the materials, it's wiped out by replacing them with new ones. So if you want your artwork to last forever, hope that someone in the distant future who thinks enough of it will go to the same trouble. Of course, the idea of guaranteeing long life for artwork is based on the notion that it may increase in value over time and warrants special attention today to ensure its life over many tomorrows.

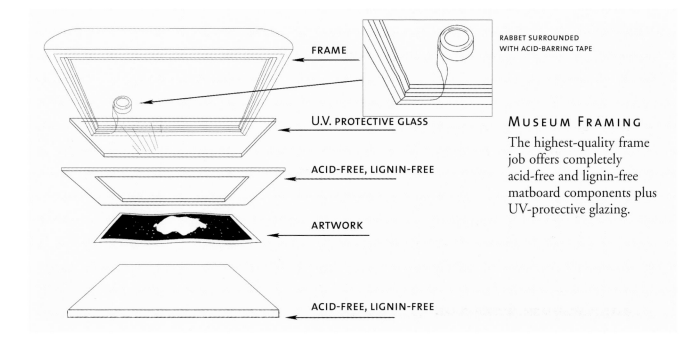

FRAME

RABBET SURROUNDED WITH ACID-BARRING TAPE

U.V. PROTECTIVE GLASS

ACID-FREE, LIGNIN-FREE

ARTWORK

ACID-FREE, LIGNIN-FREE

MUSEUM FRAMING

The highest-quality frame job offers completely acid-free and lignin-free matboard components plus UV-protective glazing.

SAFE, REGULAR FRAMING

Without conservation or museum framing, will your artwork even last into the next generation?

Rest easy. The components made for picture framing have improved dramatically in recent years. Most matboard sold today, even regular matboard, has been put through a bath of calcium carbonate to neutralize its acid content. This is sometimes referred to as acid neutralization and is considered to be so effective that some manufacturers claim it is essentially the same thing as "acid-free." The process, also called buffering, adds alkaline to the item, creating a buffer against acid. It also balances the pH of the item, resulting in a product that is sometimes referred to as "pH neutral," or "pH balanced." All of these processes render the acid harmless for a long stretch of time. How long? No one likes to say for sure.

The boards and tapes used in a regular frame job have improved significantly over the last two decades. Acid-neutralized framing components like these will protect artwork for many years.

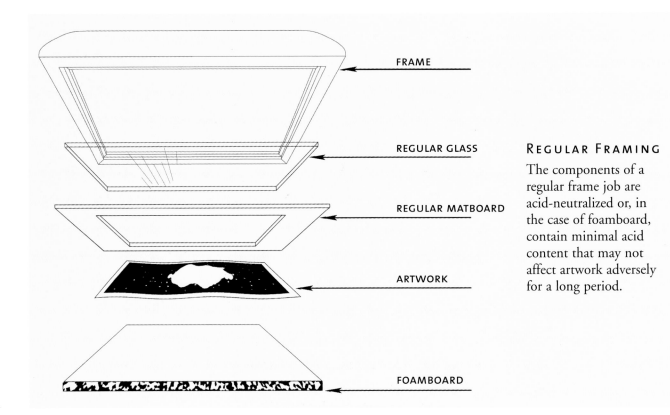

FRAME

REGULAR GLASS

REGULAR MATBOARD

ARTWORK

FOAMBOARD

REGULAR FRAMING

The components of a regular frame job are acid-neutralized or, in the case of foamboard, contain minimal acid content that may not affect artwork adversely for a long period.

PRECAUTIONS AGAINST A GHOST

The process of neutralizing framing materials started only in the mid-1980s, so the jury is still out. But one thing is sure: Components used today in framing are far safer than those used three or four decades ago, and even a standard frame job provides a considerable hedge against acid contamination. Unfortunately, most people who decide to conservation frame today are taking precautions against a ghost: the acid-laden frame job of years past.

So, should you pay more for materials that promise to be "archival quality" or "acid and lignin free"? Of course, that's up to you. But be aware that you are getting more from regular materials than you might have

thought, and weigh the question of whether you need to have your artwork last into the next century, against the question of how much you want to spend.

However—if you are going into the business of matting and framing, don't even hesitate. Go ahead and use archival materials, particularly if your client voices the least little concern about acid. The general public is as confused and anxious about this as you may have been, but many shoppers will not expect or want an explanation. They will want only to be assured that their artwork will last, so give them the peace of mind they seek by recommending top-grade archival materials.

MARY MARK, POEMS ART PUBLISHING
Art framed with Nielsen molding and Bainbridge Artcare matboards.
Photo compliments of NielsenBainbridge.

PERMANENT MOUNTING

Mounting methods fall into two broad categories: permanent and removable mounts. A permanent mount enjoys an advantage over others in that it guarantees a flat, firm mount, without buckles and waves, achieved by coating the back of the artwork with adhesive before sticking it to the matboard or foamboard mounting substrate. Since this permanent adhesion prevents the artwork from being removed from its backing at a later date, it falls far short of being a sound conservation method. By permanently sticking something to something else, you diminish its value. Therefore, permanent mounting should be reserved for those items that have little prospective long-term value, such as mass-produced posters, presentations materials that have been designed on a computer, and photographs. For such mountings, spray adhesive is a popular choice.

Spray Mount

This method, widely favored by photographers who frame their work, entails applying a uniform coat of aerosol adhesive to the back of a picture, then burnishing or rolling it onto a foamboard or matboard substrate. The process can be messy and

the spray fumes unpleasant, so work in a well-ventilated area, and wear a paper respirator. And remember, while spray adhesive is inexpensive. widely available, and easy to apply, you must be careful to buy repositionable spray adhesive. Otherwise, once the item is stuck down, it's stuck down for good. If you make the mistake of positioning it incorrectly, you are literally "stuck" with it. To get the required uniform coat with repositionable spray mount, use a fluid, side-to-side sweep of spray and avoid build up along the edges of the art by spraying beyond those edges (cover your work area with newspaper to catch oversprays). By comparison, dry mounting seems like a dream.

Dry Mount

With delightful efficiency, a good dry-mount press can take a piece of artwork and a piece of foamboard and make them one. The resulting mount is so flawless that the artwork actually appears to be printed on the substrate. Frame shops love their dry-mount presses so much that some encourage customers to order a dry mount when the archival quality of their artwork actually forbids such treatment. Dry mounting is generally not considered a conservation method. Although the materials may be acid-free, the process of affixing artwork with adhesive makes it a nonarchival choice. As with spray mounting, it should be reserved for reproducible art.

DRY MOUNTING places an adhesive-coated tissue between the artwork and the substrate. The press acts as an oven, heating the tissue and causing the adhesive to melt. Pressure is then applied to the artwork, adhering it to the substrate. A favorite of professional framers, the dry-mount press is often too costly and large for do-it-yourselfers.
Photo courtesy of Hunt Corporation SEAL® Brands.

COLD MOUNT

This may be the best choice for most do-it-yourself frame jobs. Based on adhesive-coated boards, cold mounting works by the activation of the adhesive through pressure, rather than heat, usually applied by a handheld squeegee. The mount remains repositionable until final pressure is applied. But the process does have a few drawbacks, which will be reviewed shortly. First, refer to the following photos to see how cold mounting works.

As to the limitations of cold mounting, the board itself, although rigid, is not thick enough to resist bowing and should be backed by foamboard before being placed in a frame. Cold-mounting boards also leave much to be desired when it comes to float mounting—suspending artwork against a mat blank so that the paper edges are seen. If the artwork is affixed to a cold-mounting board, it is not mounted against a mat blank; moreover, the exposed area of the mounting board is too unfinished to be a part of the presentation. Therefore, if you want to float mount using a cold-mounting board, you must cut the board to the exact size of the artwork, then mount it, with the artwork on it, to a mat blank. That may be more work than you care to do. If so, it would be easier to turn to the next option.

COLD-MOUNT boards come in large sheets that can be reduced to size as needed.
Artwork is placed face up on the board as the release paper is peeled back.

COLD-MOUNT RELEASE PAPER is placed over the artwork, which is then squeegeed down through the release paper. The artwork is fully repositionable until it is squeegeed down. This method is clean, fast, and safe.

Positionable Mounting Adhesive (PMA®)

More commonly known by its initials, PMA is a 50-foot-long sheet of paper that has one smooth side and the other coated with an inactivated adhesive. When artwork is burnished to the tacky side of the sheet, the adhesive transfers to the back of the artwork, which can then be burnished onto a matboard or foamboard substrate.

Like spray mount and unlike cold-mounting boards, PMA allows you to apply adhesive to whatever size artwork you may have with no need for trimming to accommodate the adhesive-bearing medium. As such, this choice is perfect for float mounting and is favored by photographers (and the burnishing action used will not harm most photo emulsions.)

PMA is so versatile, clean, and easy that many artists entertain using it on their watercolors, pastels, or limited-edition prints, but that idea is a serious mistake, because the artwork will be affixed permanently to its substrate. Original art requires a more archival approach, a technique and category designed to conserve artwork by allowing for safe dismounting at a future date.

Refer to the following two photos to see how to handle PMA mounting:

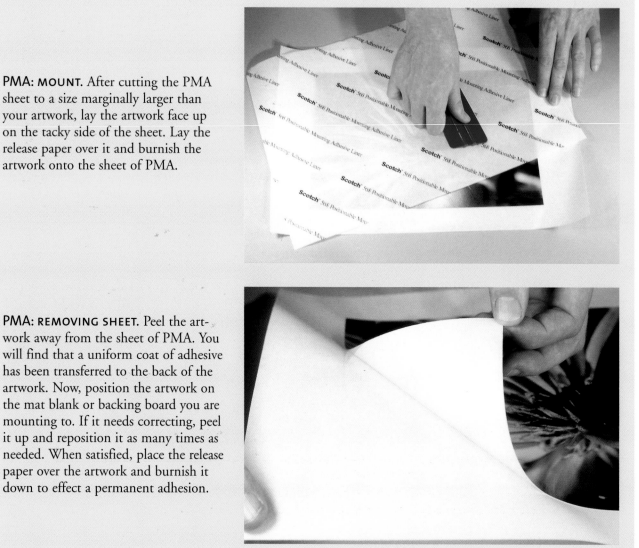

PMA: MOUNT. After cutting the PMA sheet to a size marginally larger than your artwork, lay the artwork face up on the tacky side of the sheet. Lay the release paper over it and burnish the artwork onto the sheet of PMA.

PMA: REMOVING SHEET. Peel the artwork away from the sheet of PMA. You will find that a uniform coat of adhesive has been transferred to the back of the artwork. Now, position the artwork on the mat blank or backing board you are mounting to. If it needs correcting, peel it up and reposition it as many times as needed. When satisfied, place the release paper over the artwork and burnish it down to effect a permanent adhesion.

REMOVABLE MOUNTING

Unlike the methods discussed over the past several pages, the mounting techniques that follow can be reversed. That is, the art or other materials that have been framed can be removed at some future date if the need arises. When would that be? As detailed earlier, museums do need to reframe art over the long haul, but what about the average framer? Artists who frame their own work, even nonprofessional painters, may wish to ensure its protection for family members in generations to come by enabling them to remount paintings at some future date if they so choose. Other do-it-yourself framers are just as likely to have artwork not of their own creation that they would like to remount and reframe at some point, perhaps to give it a fresh look or to coordinate with an altered room setting or to be placed in a new setting altogether. To meet those needs, here are various mounting options to consider.

HINGE MOUNTING always involves suspending artwork from tape hinges attached along the top edge of the back of the artwork. Sometimes the hinges are attached to the mounting board, as shown here, but more commonly, they are attached to the back of the mat on its border above the window, as described ahead.

HINGE MOUNT

Mounting artwork with tape has many advantages. But first, note that mounting with tape isn't called "tape mounting," as you might suspect; it's called "hinge mounting," in reference to the tabs of tape, called hinges, that hold the art in place.

Not only is this method quick, easy, and clean; it is also a good way to preserve artwork, since many quality mounting tapes are water reversible—they can be removed easily with water at the point of contact. They are also water activated; they do not become sticky until moistened.

Self-adhesive mounting tapes (those that are already sticky as they come off the roll) can be reversed with mineral spirits. Whichever you choose, be sure to use tapes made specifically for mounting artwork, as they have adhesive that can be removed.

Rather than taping along the edges of the art, hinge mounting suspends the artwork from hinges attached along the top edge of the paper. A single long strip of tape is never used, and tape is never applied to the sides or bottom of the artwork.

Hinge mounting is only effective in preserving artwork if minimal adhesive is used; two tape hinges will often suffice. Moreover, minimizing the number of hinges minimizes the restriction put on the artwork paper, allowing it to expand and contract as it absorbs and rejects moisture.

Expansion and contraction of paper is a common phenomenon with artwork, particularly with a water-based painting medium such as watercolor. To get such art to lie as flat as possible, the paper has to be allowed to "breathe."

Using as few hinges as possible promotes breathing, while taping down the artwork at each edge restricts breathing and exacerbates buckles and waves.

REINFORCED HINGE MOUNTS

The **REINFORCED T-HINGE** is made by affixing artwork to the back of a mat on its border above the window. The first tab of tape is then strengthened by placing a second tab of tape over it. The two tabs together are known as a hinge. A variation on the T-hinge is known as the **V-HINGE**. The downside to the T-hinge is that it cannot be used in any application where the edges of the paper are displayed or where the mat is spaced away from the artwork, as in an elevation presentation. For these situations the V-hinge is an alternative.

First, place your artwork on a mounting board and put the window mat over it for positioning. When you are satisfied with the alignment of the art in the window, remove the mat and set it aside. With the artwork's top edge held firmly against the mounting board, flip the artwork over so it is image side down. When you flip it over, most of it will be off the top edge of the mounting board.

When the art is flipped over, the V-hinge is concealed behind the artwork, but is near the top edge, making for a potential problem if the art is heavy and pulls out of alignment, exposing the tape. To be on the safe side, many framers who float mount prefer to use the next technique.

The **S-HINGE MOUNT** does the best job of concealing tape behind the artwork. Begin by cutting at least two slits in a mat mounting board. (Matboard is preferred for this mounting, because it is difficult to cut slits in foamboard.) Then cut two pieces of tape 4" long and prepare to feed them through each slit, adhesive side up, relative to the top edge of the mounting board. The technique is called the S-hinge because of the way the tape snakes through the slit.

Although hinge mounts are reversible, they still do put some small amount of adhesive in contact with the artwork. Arguably, the safest approach would be to avoid any contact with adhesive on the artwork at all. Mounting corners, mounting strips, and the technique of sink mounting accomplish this.

REINFORCED T-HINGE. Lay the window mat face down and place your artwork over the window, image side down. Come in 1½" from the top left corner of the art and attach a ¾"-long tape tab against the top edge of the paper, so that half of the tape is on the artwork and the other half is on the mat. Do the same at the right corner. (For artwork wider than 24", place a third tab midway between the two.) To reinforce, take another tab, this one 1½" long, and place it horizontally over the first tab to form the T. This second tab does not touch the artwork. Repeat the procedure for the remaining hinge(s).

REINFORCED V-HINGE. With the artwork flipped to the position shown, place a ¾" tab about 1½" in from the top left corner of the art, keeping half of the tape on the back of the artwork and half on the mounting board. Repeat at the other corner, then reinforce the hold of the tabs by attaching two more tapes, so one crosses each tab. The edge of the second tabs should come right to the edge of the artwork but not contact it.

REINFORCED S-HINGE mounting is based on putting two pieces of tape about two-thirds of the way through slits cut in the matboard mounting board. Attach what remains to the back of the mounting board in the area above the slit. The rest of the tape will be hanging tonguelike down the front side of the mounting board. It can be secured with a second piece of tape applied across it. Repeat the procedure for the remaining slit(s). Place your artwork over the tape and your S-hinge is complete.

Nonadhesive Mounting

The simplest method in this category harkens back to the way snapshots were once held in photo albums. The corners of the artwork are inserted into little triangular pockets that are affixed to a mounting board. Mounting corners made of clear Mylar can be purchased. They can also be made, using cotton-based drawing paper and acid-free masking tape. Cut the paper into a 1-x-2" rectangle, then fold it diagonally, bringing the longer portion of the fold across to the right and leaving a tail of about ¼". Turn the paper around and fold down the remaining strip to form a triangular pocket with a ¼" tail. Apply a tab of acid-free masking tape across the triangle to hold the pocket closed, then stick the pocket to the mounting board with a tab of adhesive transfer tape.

There is another method of this genre that is favored by photographers and artists who are willing to forgo a floated presentation. Instead of holding the artwork by securing the corners in triangular pockets, the artwork is secured along the edges, trapped between the overlapping flanges of Mylar strips. No adhesive touches the artwork, but this method cannot be used for a floated presentation—since that requires the edges of the artwork to be displayed, and nonadhesive mounting methods encroach on the edges or corners of the artwork to hold it in.

MYLAR mounting strips trap the artwork along its edges. Since a mat window then covers the strips, this method is not suited to float mounts, where the edges of the art are fully displayed.

SINK MOUNT

This method shares with other nonadhesive methods the shortcoming of being unusable for float mounts. Moreover, it is a comparatively involved process that requires careful measuring. But it offers the reward of holding original artwork that is difficult to mount, such as heavy watercolor paper, without exposing it to the debilitating effects of adhesives.

To create a sink mount, create a recess, or "sink," by assembling strips of foamboard, matboard, or watercolor paper on the face of the mounting board. The thickness of the materials you use for the strips will depend on the thickness of the item you are mounting. The recess should be about as deep as your artwork is thick. Thus, for artwork on a wood panel, foamboard strips would create a sufficient recess. For a canvas board, matboard would be the best choice.

For the strips placed along the top and bottom of the mounting board, the height of each strip is determined by subtracting the height of the artwork from the height of the frame, then dividing the difference in half. The strip width is the same as the width of the mounting board.

For the strips placed along the sides, the width of the strips is determined by subtracting the width of the artwork from the width of the frame, then dividing the difference in half. The strip height is then determined by subtracting the width of the top and bottom strips from the height of the mounting board.

Now, referring to the photos and directions in their captions:

SINK MOUNT: ASSEMBLE STRIPS. Using double-sided adhesive tape, the strips are placed so that the edge of each strip is brought flush to the edge of the mounting board, creating a recess.

SINK MOUNT: RECESS ART. Place your artwork in the recess, trapping it side to side, top to bottom.

SINK MOUNT: MATTED. When a mat is placed over the recess, the artwork is trapped front to back by overlapping edges of the mat window.
Artwork courtesy of Veronica Sebastian Potter.

ELEVATION MOUNTING: PASTEL ART

While traditional matting works for most forms of creative expression on paper, it does not for pastel, because pastel artwork is vulnerable to smudging if a mat is in direct contact with it. Also, when the work is hung, pastel particles shake loose, drift down, and collect along the beveled edge of the mat, discoloring it. The mat ruins the pastel and the pastel ruins the mat. The solution is fairly simple: Raise the mat away from the pastel.

First, prepare a mat blank on which S-hinges will be mounted. Cut slits in the blank, feed tabs of tape through the slits, and secure them to the face of the mat. Cut four strips of ⅛" foamboard, each 1" wide and as long as the mounting board to receive them. When framing pastels without a mat, it's just as important to elevate the glass away from the artwork. Cut narrow spacers ⅛" wide and place them under the lip of the frame, or use commercial spacers.

Now, with preparations complete, follow the photos and caption instructions shown:

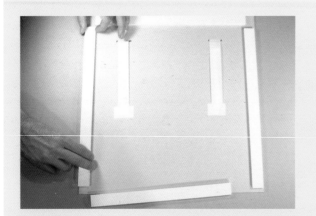

ELEVATION MOUNTING: TRANSFER TAPE. Apply adhesive transfer tape to the back of each strip and assemble them along the perimeter of the mat blank.

ELEVATION MOUNTING: POSITION ART. Dampen the mounting tape and position the artwork in the center of the mat blank, pressing it down on the mounting tape to secure it.

ELEVATION MOUNTING: MAT. Using a second piece of matboard, cut a beveled window and place it over the artwork. The window mat will rest on top of the spacers and will not contact the artwork.

VERONICA SEBASTIAN POTTER *Mandala/Spirit Catcher* **ELEVATION MOUNTING: FRAMED PASTEL.** With glass over the window mat and the entire stack inserted, since there is an additional ⅛" thickness in the stack due to the spacers, use a frame with a rabbet depth of at least ⅝" to allow for it.

MOUNTING NEEDLEWORK

This project begins with blocking and proceeds through securing and matting needlework. Blocking is required because during stitching, some needlework usually pulls out of shape and is no longer square; that is, the corners do not form perfect right angles and the opposite edges are not parallel to each other. Blocking is needed to stretch the item back to its proper shape.

Blocking is done on a thick board; sometimes hardboard or plywood is used, but Upson board is most common because it is found at many art-supply stores and is somewhat easier to cut—which is not to imply you should anticipate a breezy experience. Upson board is a ⅜"-thick gray board that requires repeated passes of a utility knife to penetrate it. Take your time. Mark out the board to your frame size and align a metal straight-edge or T-square along the marked line. Score lightly to begin, and don't try to plow your blade through in just a few passes or you will end up with a jagged edge.

After preparing the blocking board, if it is needlepoint work, as shown in the demonstration that follows, its open-mesh canvas should be moistened to relax, or stretch, it back into square. Traditionally, this is done by misting or steaming, but commercial relaxants are now available for this purpose.

After the needlepoint has been relaxed, lay it face up on the Upson board and align one edge square; fasten it to the board with push pins along the edge. Stretch the opposite edge across and pin, then do the top and bottom borders. Let the piece dry before removing it from the stretching board.

Your best bet for a mounting board is two pieces of ⅛"-thick acid-free foamboard taped together. The soft center makes it easy to insert the straight pins you will use for mounting the needlepoint canvas. Cut the foamboard so it's ⅛" smaller on each dimension than your frame size to allow for the thickness of the canvas as it is stretched around the edges of the board.

Now, refer to the photos and directions in the captions that follow:

NEEDLEWORK MOUNT: BATTING. Before placing the needlework on the mounting board, tape a piece of polyester batting to the middle of the mounting board. Batting promotes air circulation around the artwork to fend off rot.

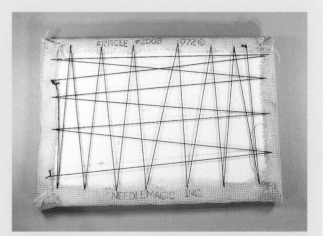

NEEDLEWORK MOUNT: STRETCH. This is the back of the foamboard after the needlepoint has been secured to it, face up, with pins inserted ½" apart around the edges to keep the needlepoint taut. Now the edges are folded over to the back, as shown, and sewn in a criss-cross pattern.

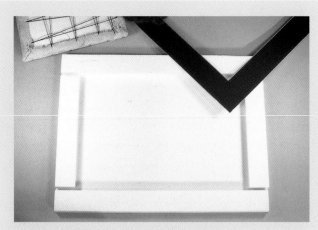

NEEDLEWORK MOUNT: ELEVATE. When placing a mat over needlework, raise the mat with narrow strips of foamboard taped to a mat blank, near its outer edges. This puts the mat on a level with the needlework. While glass is not usually placed over needlepoint, if you plan to glaze over embroidery, for example, stack at least two strips of foamboard to keep the glass away from the stitched art.

NEEDLEWORK MOUNT: INSERT. Once the foamboard strips are assembled, the mounted needlework will nest in the recess created by the strips.

NEEDLEWORK MOUNT: FRAMED. With a mat placed over the strips and a frame added, your needlework is ready to be hung for display.

MOUNTING THREE-DIMENSIONAL OBJECTS

A challenging project for the do-it-yourself framer is mounting three-dimensional objects in a box-type frame. It might be a collection of like items such as seashells, or it could be an arrangement of disparate items or mementos—such as the example in our demonstration—that have meaning only for the person who wants them mounted for display.

To mount such items in an object box, sometimes called a shadow box, prepare your mounting surface first, using a sheet of ³⁄₁₆"-thick foamboard covered with fabric. Black velvet is the choice used in our example; the objects you assemble may be displayed to better advantage on a light or bright background of another fabric texture.

Size your foamboard, making it ¼" smaller than the interior of the box you will use. Place the fabric over your foamboard. Arrange the objects on it as you want them to be displayed. Some objects require preparation to the foamboard, such as items to be imbedded before pinning; others are not mounted until after the fabric is stretched and pinned to the foamboard.

OBJECT BOX: PIN. At 1½" spaces, pin along the top edge first, working from one corner to the midpoint, then go to the bottom edge, diagonally.

OBJECT BOX: IMBED. To imbed an object like this cup, the fabric was first folded back, so a hole could be cut in the foamboard (a bit larger than the cup). After stretching and pinning the fabric halfway along the top and bottom of the foamboard, locate the hole through the velvet and cut two intersecting slits there with a razor blade. Imbed the cup about a third of the way down. Secure it with a nail inserted through the back of the foamboard and held in place with electrical tape. Finish pinning the fabric so that it is taut for the next step.

OBJECT BOX: SEALER. To mount a ball, fold back the fabric and gouge out a small crater in the foamboard. After pinning the fabric taut again, use a razor blade to cut a hole in the fabric over the crater. Squeeze silicon rubber sealer into the hole and press the ball into it.

OBJECT BOX: ACRYLIC HOLDER. An acrylic holder for the knife has a post-and-nut system. The knife is held by a clamp that closes the blade near the hasp. The post is then secured by a nut at the back of the foamboard. Acrylic gun holders, spoon holders, and coin holders are also available through internet framing suppliers.

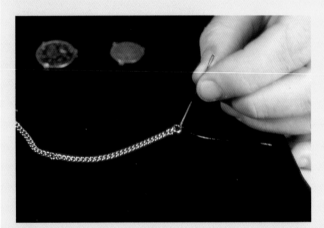

OBJECT BOX: SEWN ITEMS. To mount loose, lightweight items such as this chain, after stretching and pinning the fabric, use a pilot needle and invisible thread to sew the item to the foamboard, which is surprisingly easy to do. Sew it at two or three points around the object. Pull the thread tight and tape it on the back of the foamboard to secure it. The coins shown have been secured with acrylic holders that are calibrated to common coin sizes.

OBJECT BOX: PANEL. Using the object box you prepared in "Step 4, Preparing Your Materials," or using a store-bought object box, place your fully mounted board in the box. Use strips of matboard to panel the inside of the box.

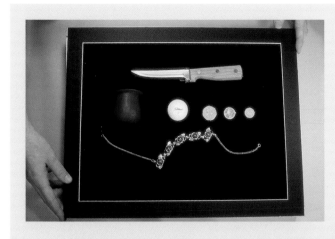

OBJECT BOX: MAT, GLAZE, AND FRAME. Place a mat over the object box with the items now mounted in it. The mat should be the same size as the box, with borders wide enough to cover the exposed wood of the box, but not so wide that they encroach too much on the presentation area. Cut your glazing to the same size as the box, and place the glazing over the matted box. You are now ready to place a frame over your object box, much as you would place a lid on a shoebox. Use a frame that is the same size as the box. Instructions for securing the frame on the object box are found in "Step 8: Glazing, Installing, and Hanging Framed Art."

DAVID LOGAN
Memories of the Orient

This completely framed object box shows how a colorful mat and gold frame
coordinate the items in the display and heighten its overall appeal.

Art framed with Nielsen molding and Bainbridge Artcare matboards.

Photo compliments of NielsenBainbridge.

ASSEMBLING FRAMES

Whether you have fashioned your own molding out of lumber, acquired commercial molding in length from a wholesaler, or purchased chopped and routed molding from a frame supplier through mail order or the internet, you still have ahead of you the task of assembling the frame. What you can anticipate in terms of effort depends on the stage the molding is in when you start.

For example, if you have created your own molding out of lumber, you still have to miter cut it before clamping it to be joined. On the other hand, if you've bought your molding from a mail order or internet supplier, it's already miter cut and routed for easy joining without clamps or vices.

Of these and other possible choices, perhaps the easiest frame of all to assemble is a metal sectional frame, so let's begin there.

METAL SECTIONAL FRAMES

Packaged in presized sections in pairs, a metal sectional frame is assembled from two pairs, each pair sold separately. For example, if you want a frame that measures 16 x 20", buy a pair of 16" sections and combine them with a pair of 20" sections; for a frame that measures 11 x 16", buy a pair of 11" sections and a pair of 16" sections—and so on. Both ends of each section are miter cut; that is, cut at a 45-degree angle so that when pressed together they form a 90-degree corner. The back of each section is extruded with a channel.

Assembly consists of inserting a stack of two L-shaped brackets into the extruded channel of one section. The top bracket in each stack has two screws in it. By turning the screws, the brackets are forced apart, exerting pressure on the interior of the extrusion. The adjoining section is then slid onto the other arm of each bracket and tightened. By tightening the screws on each side of each bracket, the corners are held tight and the frame is assembled. Before attaching the last section, slide in the components (artwork, matboard, foamboard, and glazing). Assemble the last section now, and your metal frame is complete.

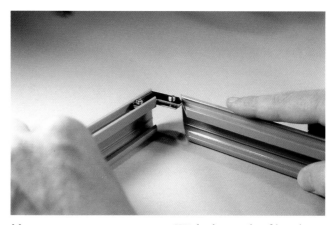

METAL FRAME ASSEMBLAGE. With the stack of brackets in place, the adjoining section is slid on and tightened.

SARAH BACCI
Grace

A stark-white mat and simple black frame allow the viewer's eye to go directly to the focal point of the presentation, the dramatic black-and-white photo.

Like metal sectional frames, wood sectional frames are packaged in pairs of full-inch lengths, which can be combined to make a variety of frame sizes. Like metal sectional frames, they are miter cut at a 45-degree angle to form 90-degree corners, and are equipped with a system for joining that requires minimal tools. But whereas the one tool needed for joining metal sectionals is a screwdriver, the tool needed for joining wood sectionals is a hammer. In addition, wood sectionals require wood glue.

At the back of each wood section, at each mitered end, there is a channel routed into the wood. When the miters of two sections are brought together to form a corner, the routed channels align, forming a continuous channel, usually in the shape of a V or a bow tie. Included with the frame are plastic pegs in the same shape, which can be pressed into the channels to hold the frame together. These pegs are supposedly easily inserted with only thumb pressure, but often have to be coaxed with a hammer.

Assembling wood sectional frames is simple. Coat two adjoining miter faces with a thin layer of wood glue, press the miters together, and insert a peg. Wipe away excess glue at the join, then repeat the procedure for each remaining corner.

Let the glue dry for at least twenty minutes before attempting to load components into the frame.

WOOD FRAME ASSEMBLING. Press the frame miters together to form a corner; the routed channels will line up. Insert the peg. A hammer may be needed to push it all the way down.

CUTTING AND JOINING LENGTH MOLDING

With chopped and routed frames being so easy and inexpensive to join, it's hard to understand why someone would want to make an investment in costly joining equipment. As detailed in the earlier "Materials and Equipment" chapter, buying length molding and cutting and assembling it is a costly and complicated process for do-it-yourselfers. But for readers who own a miter saw, are more experienced with framing, and may sometimes purchase molding in lengths, here is some useful guidance.

When placing molding in a miter saw, there are several ways to mess it up. If you do, you will know it when you press two sections together to form a corner and discover that the rabbet on one section is opposite the rabbet on the other. To avoid such a mistake, set the miter saw at 90 degrees and cut the long stick of molding into four sections, each one slightly longer than what will be needed for each section of the frame.

Then refer to the pictures and captions that follow.

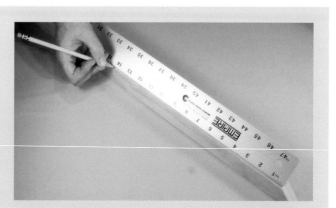

LENGTH MOLDING: FIRST CUT. Set your miter saw at 45 degrees and place the first section against the fence with the molding facing up and the rabbet turned toward you. Miter cut one end at 45 degrees.

LENGTH MOLDING: SECOND CUT. Place the molding back in the saw and align the mark just made. Turn the saw on its rotator to 135 degrees (45 degrees to the right) and make your next cut. You now have one section of frame molding complete. For each section remember to begin cutting with the saw at 45-degrees. Place the stick in the saw with molding face up and the rabbet turned toward you. After cutting, turn the saw to 135 degrees to make the second cut.

LENGTH MOLDING: COMPLETE. Lay the completed section back to back with the remaining uncut length of molding. Using the completed section as a guide, measure and mark the second section so you will know exactly where to align the cut.

LENGTH MOLDING: MEASURE. With the molding out of the miter saw, measure down its length. Start your measurement at the inside edge of the miter cut and measure the length of the section you want to produce, plus ⅛" to allow for the thickness of the blade. Mark the molding.

After cutting, sand the rough edges. If the molding needs to be stained or painted, and you haven't already done so, do so now. If your molding is already stained, hold the mitered ends together and see if you have a noticeable seam.

If you do, you will have to use touch-up inks to blend it with the color of the molding and conceal the seam. Now you are ready to join.

A corner clamp is used to secure a frame corner so the miters are pressed together. Four clamps are needed to clamp all four corners simultaneously. As with the peg-and-channel system, wood glue is used to bond the corners before nailing. Spread a thin coat of the glue on one miter face. Bring in the adjoining section and clamp the two miter faces together, then wipe away excess glue that squeezes out at the join.

With the two sections clamped together, hammer two brads through the long section into the end of the short section. Repeat the procedure for the remaining four corners. Allow one hour for the glue to dry.

A miter vice works in much the same way as a corner clamp, holding two miters together for nailing. Those who work with miter vices tend to go slower because they can only glue and nail one corner at a time and must wait for the glue to dry before moving on to the next corner.

VERONICA SEBASTIAN POTTER
The Moon Which Remains Forever

With careful cutting, creative multiple matting that has a crisp, professional look like this can be easily achieved by the do-it-yourself framer.

N. GREGORY, DELJOU ART GROUP

Art framed with Nielsen molding and Bainbridge Artcare matboards.

Photo by Peter Paige, compliments of NielsenBainbridge.

GLAZING, INSTALLING, & HANGING FRAMED ART

Tidying things up and putting everything into the frame probably seems like an easy part of the process and hardly worth taking up a whole chapter. But this stage is more time-consuming than you may think, and because it appears simple, it's more frustrating when it drags on—particularly if you're a perfectionist. But as long as you plan ahead by knowing what to expect, you will be ready for it. So if you are a perfectionist, outfit yourself with the tools that will help smooth out the rough spots for you.

Finally, be prepared to surrender perfection for sanity. Not everything has to stand up to inspection under a magnifying glass. But even if you are not of an exacting nature, glazing has been known to make perfectionists of the most flexible people—glazing in general, and in particular, cleaning glass. So let us begin there.

GLAZING

At this stage, your glazing has been sized to your frame, or you bought it that way, and all that remains is to clean it before it goes into the frame. You wipe it down with a quality glass cleaner and hold it up to the light. It seems clear enough. But just as you are slippng it into the frame, you notice a few smudges. So you wipe again. Now you check it out more carefully, tilting it this way and that to catch the light and you notice even more smears than had first appeared. You wipe and check it again. This goes on for some time until you find you've gone through more than half a bottle of glass cleaner. Now it probably oc-

curs to you that there's got to be a better way to clean glass. Well, there is—but it is not necessarily faster, nor in the short term, anyway, cheaper.

Make your own glass cleaner. Into a pint of water mix 4 fluid ounces of denatured alcohol and a half-teaspoon of dish detergent. The magic of this solution is the alcohol's ability to dissolve grease, coupled with the static-fighting properties of the detergent. This effective home-made solution will spare you having to wipe the glass repeatedly with commercial glass cleaner. But if you want it to work, prepare to be patient. Your steps to success, as described in the following two photos and captions, are:

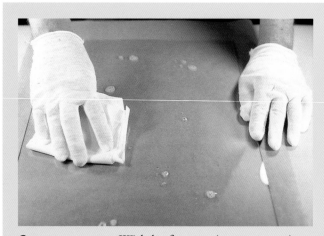 

CLEANING GLASS: With kraft paper (or newspaper) placed under the glass, apply the solution on one side and spread it around with a paper towel. Wait a moment to let the alcohol break down oily smudges. Then wipe the glass, but do not wipe it dry. With the glass still moist, flip it over to wet the second side. Again, spread the solution and wait for the alcohol to go to work. Wipe, leaving the glass moist, then turn it back to the first side. Wipe it until it is nearly dry, then let it air dry the rest of the way. (Dry wiping glass can cause static build-up that attracts dust and lint.) Turn the glass to the second side, wipe again, and let it air dry. Wear cotton gloves when cleaning glass to avoid smudging.

HANDLING GLASS: A glass pick-up stick is a handy way to lift glass without touching it. Using a paper towel, wipe the glass, working from the center outward to avoid shredding the paper on the edges of the glass. Otherwise, you might wind up with tiny flakes of paper clinging to the surface. They cling because of static electricity, which is made worse by wiping a dry paper towel across the surface—so once the glass is well along to drying, stop wiping.

If you glaze with acrylic instead of glass, static electricity is an even greater problem. Never wipe acrylic with a paper towel, not only because of static electricity, but because acrylic is very vulnerable to scratching and should only be cleaned with a soft flannel cloth and mild soapy water or a plastic cleaner with an antistatic agent.

SPACERS

In glazing, most often glass lies atop mat, which separates the glass away from the artwork. But when you are not using a mat, spacers should be placed between the glazing and the artwork to separate them so that condensation will not occur under the glass, causing blotches and wrinkling on the artwork.

To separate glazing from artwork, you will need spacers. As described in the chapter about materials, commercial spacers are long plastic strips that are narrower than the lip of the frame and thick enough to ensure proper separation. You can purchase commercial spacers, available in a choice of thickness, but you might want to economize by making your own from matboard. It is not difficult, particularly if you have a good mat cutter with a mat-guide measuring system.

Typically, the lip of the frame (that part that encroaches onto the edge of the glass) is ¼"; you would cut your foamboard strips at a width of ³⁄₁₆" so they will be hidden well under the lip of the frame. Place a strip of foamboard at least 1¼" wide into your mat cutter with the guide set narrower than the strip by ³⁄₁₆". So if the foamboard is 1¼", set the mat guide for 1¹⁄₁₆". Now all that is exposed for cutting is ³⁄₁₆", and there may be a tendency for the 90-degree cutting head to tip off the narrow edge foamboard as you cut. To give added support for the cutting head, take another strip of foamboard and tape it flush up against the one being cut. Now the cutting head will glide flat as it cuts. The foamboard strips do not have to be the full length of the frame sides, but they should be at least half as long.

After cutting the spacers, use ¼"-wide adhesive transfer tape to adhere them to the face of the backing board along each edge. At ¹⁄₁₆", the adhesive will be slightly wider than the spacers, so you'll have to roll the excess around the sides with your thumbs; that, plus positioning the spacers, can be tricky. Indeed, at this point, commercial spacers might seem a worthwhile investment, but knowing how to make them yourself is a good alternative for the cost-conscious framer.

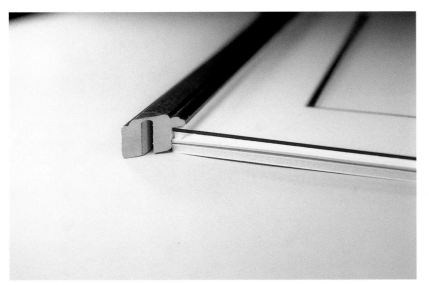

Making spacers out of foamboard is not difficult; getting them in position under the lip of the frame is a bit more of a challenge. Be sure to apply the spacers along each edge so they will be concealed under the lip of the frame when it is in place. When you place glass over the artwork, the spacers will separate it nicely from the art.

INSTALLING THE ARTWORK SANDWICH

The stack of components you place in a frame is called the **ARTWORK SANDWICH.** In the case of mat-free framing, it's a stack of backing board, artwork, spacers, and glass; with matted artwork, it's backing board, artwork, mat, and glass. When the mat is separated from the artwork, as is commonly done with pastels or charcoals, it's backing board, artwork, spacers, mat, and glass.

Let me caution here that even before you put your artwork sandwich together, you should know what kind of frame you will use to contain it. That topic will be explored shortly when we get to "frame fitting."

Regardless of the components that comprise the sandwich, you have the option of taping the edges to hold everything together neatly and to seal the artwork against dust. It is not absolutely necessary to do so if your sandwich fits neatly into the frame, and if the frame is clean to begin with, dust should not be a problem. But if you want to

ensure a completely dust-free home for the art, seal the edges of the sandwich with pressure-sensitive tape. Avoid using water-activated tape as it will not stick to the glass. If conservation is not a major concern, masking tape can be used. If conservation is a concern, use a pressure-sensitive neutral pH product, such as linen tape or frame-sealing tape.

Before applying tape, make sure all components are dry. Any moisture trapped inside the sealed sandwich can damage the artwork. In applying tape, be sure that it does not encroach more than ¼" onto the face of the glass.

Taping the sandwich is one of those areas where additional time and expense can be avoided if you are willing to lower your sights in terms of perfection. By not taping the sandwich, a few specks of dust may find their way inside the glass or onto the surface of the art, but it is unlikely that the dust will be so egregious that you will notice it without having to look for it.

To prevent dust from penetrating the sandwich, tape the edges of the sandwich. The lip of the frame will overlap and conceal the tape, but only if the tape extends less than ¼" onto the face of the glass. The amount the tape encroaches onto the bottom of the sandwich is not an issue. Run the tape all the way to the corners.

FRAME FITTING

Installing artwork in a frame is known as "frame fitting," and it's no misnomer. One of the most frustrating situations you'll encounter in picture framing is to reach this stage and find that your sandwich will not fit, and not because you figured your frame size incorrectly. Length and width are dimensions you paid close attention to while measuring, but in all likelihood, the problem stems from another dimension: depth. Specifically, how deep is your frame? And will your artwork sandwich fit into it?

ADJUSTING THE SANDWICH FOR A METAL FRAME

This problem is best illustrated in the case of metal frames. You have just assembled three sides, and now you start to slide the sandwich into the open end before putting the fourth side on, but the sandwich is too thick, and it will not slide in. If you remember that you have only about ⅝" of clearance in a metal frame, you will avoid the problem. A typical sandwich comprised of foamboard, artwork, a double mat, and glass comes to about ⅜" and ought to slide in with no difficulty. But introduce a triple mat and a ³⁄₁₆" spacer to the sandwich, as you would for a pastel, and you're stymied. If you plan ahead, that will never happen.

When you are likely to produce a thick sandwich, try to shave some of that bulk by minimizing some component thicknesses. There is not much you can do with matboard or glass, but you can opt for ⅛-thick foamboard, rather than ³⁄₁₆", and spacers of ⅛", rather than ³⁄₁₆" or ¼". Doing so will knock at least ⅛ out of the total sandwich and allow it to slide in easily.

Don't worry about making the sandwich too thin. In a metal frame you may end up with a loose front-to-back fit of the sandwich, but manufacturers of metal frames anticipate that and provide narrow metal strips, known as spring clips, to take up the gap.

Spring clips can be slipped in between the extrusion and the backing board to fill the excess space in a metal frame.
These narrow metal strips are provided by the manufacturers of metal frames. Here, a screwdriver is used to help push the clip in place.

Securing the Sandwich in a Wood Frame

If the artwork sandwich is not thick enough to fill a wood frame, don't worry. Since you load the sandwich in the recess, or rabbet, at the back of the frame, and since you secure it in place with brads or points inserted at a right angle into the rabbet, if the sandwich doesn't fill to the top, it's a good thing—because it allows you to get at the rabbet. The brads or metal tabs, called points, are inserted just above the back of the sandwich, making for a tight pack. With the correct tools, the process is quick and easy—but some tools are easier than others.

BRADS are small wire nails that can be tapped in with a hammer, the least expensive way of securing the sandwich in a wood frame. However, the process is awkward and the bulk of the hammer requires you to drive the brads at a clumsy angle. Try using a pair of long-nose pliers to hold the brads as you tap. Some framers elect to push the brads in with a tool called a brad pusher, a cigarette-length cylinder with a socket at one end that fits over the head of the nail to drive it in. But the application requires some strength, and the brad pusher is not so easy to come by.

A NAIL SET is another method, but the process is awkward and the tool can slip off in use. If you are working with a hardwood frame, forget it, because it will brook no interference from a hand-squeezed nail, which means that you will have to use a power drill to make a pilot hole for the nail. You could up the ante by purchasing a brad squeezer, a tool that works like a vise to squeeze the nail into the frame, and with enough sweat you might even be able to conquer hardwood. But now we are moving away from cheap alternatives. It is time to step back and evaluate things.

Unlike many areas of picture framing, in the area of frame fitting, the trade-off between efficiency and cost is justified. The gulf that lies between fumbling with brads and effortlessly driving a point is more than commensurate with the difference in cost. Also, when you reach this stage in the process, you can see the artwork in the frame and are eager to be finished. Investing in a system to secure the contents quickly is one of the best framing investments you will make. Brads are a pain. So what is better?

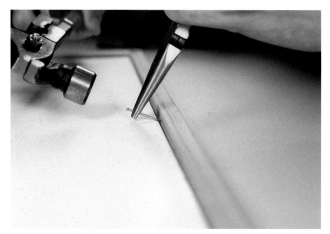

When using brads to secure the artwork sandwich in the rabbet recess at the back of a wood frame, it helps to hold the brad with a pair of long-nose pliers as you tap it in place with a hammer.

Another alternative is to squeeze the brad into the rabbet with a nail set, a piece of hardware that looks like the leg of a coffee table in miniature. The flat side of the nail set is placed against the nail head. Pressure is applied by squeezing in on the nail as you press on the outside of the frame with your thumb.

POINTS are better. If you are going to spend money, spend it in the right place. Having said that, budget point inserting is not much better than brad pushing. Pushing is pushing. A *point pusher* is a handle with a socket at one end; a *glazier's point* is a pointed metal tab. The glazier's point is fitted into the socket and you push. Unlike a nail set, the point pusher holds the point securely and can't slip off. Still, the process feels crude, and hardwoods will again be an obstacle.

The **FRAMER'S TOOL,** a step up in sophistication, is for those who are willing to invest a bit more. A viselike affair in the same vein as a brad squeezer, it vises the point into the rabbet with the squeeze of a handle. Somewhat tedious to use, this tool at least incorporates elementary mechanics into its design.

The **POINT DRIVER** is, however, the ultimate in inserting points. It is leaps and bounds ahead of its nearest rival. Able to stand up to hardwoods with authority, the point driver fires a point with pneumaticlike force at the squeeze of a handle. Reminiscent of a nail gun, the tool is placed against the back of the loaded sandwich. The nose is then pressed against the rabbet and the point is fired.

Within seconds, the sandwich is secured in the frame. While not cheap, a point driver is still only about a third the cost of a 40½" mat cutter, and a fraction of the cost of precision frame-making equipment.

For the home picture framer seeking a balance of efficiency and economy, the point driver is a worthwhile investment.

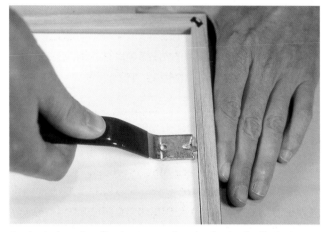

A glazier's point fits into a socket at the end of a point pusher, then the tip of the point is placed against the rabbet of the frame and pushed in. The point pusher holds the glazier's point securely in place.

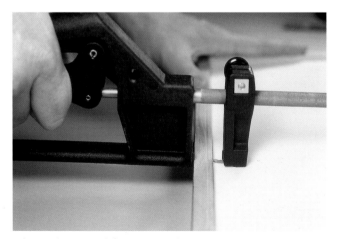

The aptly named framer's tool is a viselike device that drives the point into the rabbet with the squeeze of a handle.

The most sophisticated tool for the job, the point driver is placed against the back of the loaded sandwich. With the nose up against the rabbet, the point is fired in with great ease.

When the Sandwich Is Too Thick for a Wood Frame

Unfortunately, a point driver only works if you can get the nose of it against the rabbet of the frame. In those instances where the artwork sandwich is too thick for the recess and therefore sits above the back of the frame, other measures are called for.

If the sandwich is only marginally thicker than the recess is deep, and foamboard has been used as a backing, the problem can be solved by crushing the edges of the foamboard with the shaft of a screwdriver. When you place the sandwich in the recess, the backing should be collapsed sufficiently along the edges to allow the nose of the point driver access to the rabbet.

OFF-SET CLIPS come into play when the sandwich is too thick even for the crushing method. Known alternatively as MIRROR CLIPS and available in most hardware stores, these small metal bars have two right-angle bends forming offsetting flat ends between a vertical upright. One of the flat ends has a hole in it. This end is screwed into the back of the frame. The vertical upright is placed against the side of the sandwich, and the opposing flat end overlaps the back of it.

The methods described above are helpful, but when it comes to framing art on paper, resorting to them need never occur if you plan ahead. When you get your frame, measure the rabbet depth (the depth of the recess) and make sure that the sandwich you assemble is able to fit it.

When the artwork sandwich is too thick to fit into the frame, before placing it in the recess, crush the edges of the foamboard by rolling the shaft of a screwdriver over it.

When the sandwich is too thick for the crushing method, offset clips are useful. One end is screwed into the back of the frame; the other grips the sandwich. They come in three offsets, ⅛", ¼", and ½".

INSTALLING STRETCHED CANVAS IN A FRAME

After lowering a stretched canvas into a frame, you will probably find that the stretcher bars are seated above the back of the frame. Some frames are deep enough to accept stretched canvas, but the selection is limited, so many framers end up having to fit to shallower frames. The most obvious approach is to drive nails at an angle through the stretcher bars and into the rabbet, but this is a clumsy business and restricts the natural expansion and contraction of the stretched canvas and can cause problems later should it become necessary to remove the painting from the frame.

Offset clips can be used when the stretcher bars are seated less than ½" above the back of the frame. **CANVAS CLIPS** are an easy alternative and snap into place, overlapping the stretcher bars and holding them in place with pointed prongs and spring tension. They are particularly good when the stretcher bars are flush with the back of the frame.

INSTALLING A FRAME OVER AN OBJECT BOX

Some object boxes, such as those that you buy ready-made, are frames unto themselves. Other object boxes, such as those that you make yourself, are only presentation trays and must have a frame installed over them. Almost without exception, this type of object box is deeper than the frame that fits over it. To secure a frame on such an object box, lay the frame face down and attach screw eyes to the back of the frame, one on each side, placing each within ¼" of the recess. Place the frame over the object box, then insert a straight screw through each screw eye and screw them into the side of the box.

When an oil painting on its stretchers is too thick to fit into a frame, canvas clips may be used. They snap into place, overlapping the stretcher bars and holding them in place with pointed prongs and spring tension.

Dust Cover for Art on Paper

Many framers like to attach a brown-paper dust cover to the back of the frame. The dust cover is both functional and cosmetic. It keeps out dust and moisture and provides a clean, professional look for the back of the frame. Dust covers are usually made from inexpensive kraft paper, the same paper that is used for wrapping packages.

First, cut a sheet of kraft paper larger than the frame. Next, apply white glue to the back of the frame. While the glue sets, dampen the kraft paper. Place the frame, glue side down, on the paper; be sure the glue is contacting the paper uniformly. Now wait. As the paper dries it will shrink, pulling itself as tight as a drum. When dry, you will trim the excess, with the frame lying face down, using an X-Acto knife and straightedge.

First, crease the paper along the edge of the frame so you will be able to clearly discern where to cut. Then score lightly and, if necessary, more than once. Don't bear down. If you do, the knife may walk out from the straightedge and give you a jagged, unprofessional cut. To avoid this, some framers prefer to use a tool called a dust-cover trimmer. Equipped with a guide, it keeps the blade at a uniform distance from the frame edge while cutting.

The use of a dust cover is quite common for art on paper, but not mandatory. Attaching it is easy; refer to the three photos and captions that follow:

DUST COVER: GLUE. Apply white glue to the back of the frame, spreading it evenly with a paper towel.

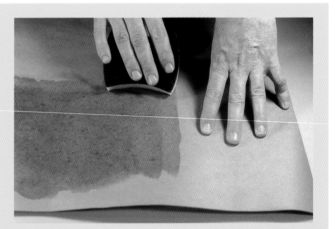

DUST COVER: DAMPEN PAPER. While the glue sets, with a sponge, dampen the kraft paper you had cut to a size larger than the frame.

DUST COVER: TRIM. After the paper has been pressed firmly on the frame and the glue has been allowed to dry, causing the paper to shrink and become taut, the excess paper is trimmed away, often with an X-Acto knife. Here, a tool known as a dust-cover trimmer is employed for the job.

Dust Cover for Art on Canvas

To what degree you should go to protect the back of a framed canvas depends on the environment in which it will be displayed. A major concern for canvas is adequate air circulation, and this is best accomplished by not covering the back at all. Dust and insects are another issue, but you will have to ask yourself if they are a real problem where the art will be hanging and if you need a dust cover at all.

If you do want one, the fastest method is to cut a sheet of foamboard the same size as the stretched canvas and lop off the corners to promote air circulation. The foamboard is then attached to the stretcher bar with brads. A more elaborate approach is to attach kraft paper and outfit it with a small screened window for air circulation. The window is cut with an X-Acto knife following the contours of a 2 x 3" template made from a piece of scrap matboard. A small piece of screening is taped over the window to thwart insects.

The two photos at right depict the methods just described.

FOAMBOARD DUST COVER: Made of foamboard cut to size and tacked onto the back of the frame with brads, this method is quick and easy.

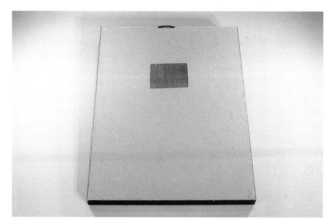

KRAFT-PAPER DUST COVER. Using a template made of matboard, a window is cut in a sheet of Kraft paper and a screen taped over it. The paper is then attached to the back of the frame.

WHAT THEY DON'T SEE *CAN* SAVE YOU MONEY

It always amazes me how eager home framers are to attach a dust cover, even after they find out it's optional. While the dust cover can go some way to keeping out dust and moisture, if you took the trouble to seal the edges of your artwork sandwich, its function is superfluous. And if dust is not a problem that's been plaguing you, it's probably overkill. As a cosmetic consideration, however, the appeal of the dust cover is powerful. It puts the finishing touch on your work and says that, even if you are not a professional, you frame like one. Home framers love dust covers.

But if you are trying to save time and money doing your own picture framing, this is one area where you can cut costs. If you are framing for yourself and the destination of your work is your own walls, probably nobody will see the back of the frame but you. If you are framing for friends or family, you are proba-

bly doing it for a lot less than the local frame shop charges, so it's easy to justify skipping the dust cover as a cost-saving measure. And while the absence of a dust cover might at first give the recipient pause, once the frame is hanging, that deficiency is quickly forgotten.

And what do you save by leaving it off? Well, aside from the time it takes to attach the dust cover, you save the cost of the materials and tools needed to put it on. Perhaps you already have them, but if you don't, you skip the cost of an X-Acto knife, a straightedge, and the kraft paper itself which, foot by foot, is cheap, but may only be available in large rolls.

Attaching a dust cover may still be something you'll want to do, but you do have an option here—one that can take a bite out of your framing time and costs.

ATTACHING HANGING HARDWARE

After the contents of the frame are installed and the dust cover is in place, it's time to attach the hanging hardware. For lightweight wood frames that are 8 x 10" or smaller, pressure-sensitive adhesive hangers or sawtooth clips are an economical choice.

The familiar **ADHESIVE HANGERS,** which are patches of high-density polyethylene, have a hole for hanging and are quick and easy to use, but are a bit precarious for anything heavier than one pound. **SAWTOOTH CLIPS** can bear more weight. These narrow, serrated bars are nailed into the middle back of the frame. The serrations allow marginal side-to-side shifts of the artwork on a nail for straight hanging, but if the clip is not centered, straightening can still be a problem.

You may find the tiny nails clumsy to work with, and once you've groped along a wall blindly trying find a nail with the clip, you'll understand why sawtooth clips should be reserved for smaller framed pieces.

For framed pieces of 8 x 10" or larger, **HANGING WIRE** is the way to go, one common method of installing being with **SCREW EYES.** When working with soft woods, screw eyes can be started into the frame by hand and finished with a screwdriver or an awl inserted through the loop for turning. One drawback to screw eyes is that they protrude from the back of the frame and can mar the wall. **STRAP HANGERS** (also called **MIRROR HANGERS**) are sturdy metal flanges with D-shaped rings at one end. They attach to the frame with separate screws and have the advantage of lying flat against the back of the frame. The wire is then looped through the D-ring and tied off.

No matter which devices you choose to attach the hanging wire, they cannot be screwed into a hardwood frame by hand and holes will have to be predrilled to accommodate them. This is another good reason to steer clear of hardwoods such as oak, maple, and walnut when purchasing picture frames.

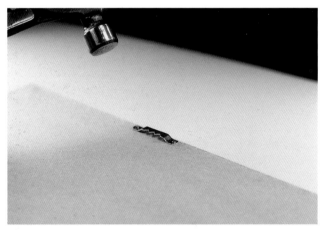

Sawtooth clips allow for marginal side-to-side shifts of the artwork on the nail for straight hanging.

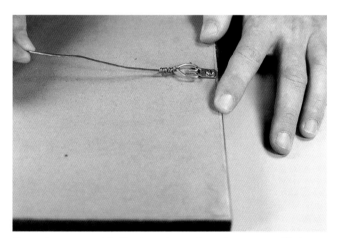

Strap hangers with D-rings have the advantage of lying flat against the back of the frame.

In most cases, you needn't fuss over the positioning of the devices for tying the hanging wire. Just eyeball a position about a third of the way down on each side of the frame and screw them in. If you are slightly off and the two devices are not precisely across from each other, you can compensate by sliding the wire along the hanger on the wall until the picture hangs straight. Feed the wire through the hangers and evaluate the amount of slack. The vertex of the wire should come to about an inch from the top edge of the frame, but if there is any question of excess slack after tying off, you may want to subtract ¼" to allow for it.

Tying the wire is a matter of feeding it through the hanger twice and coiling it tightly around itself four or five times. Picture-framing wire is made of braids of many smaller wires and it is not uncommon for them to fray and cut your fingers. Plastic-coated framing wire eliminates the problem and can be bought at a nominal extra cost.

When the framed piece is exceptionally large or heavy, the installation of extra hangers is warranted. Screw eyes should be installed in the rabbet at the bottom of the frame about a quarter of the way in from each corner as well as on either side of the recess about a quarter of the way down from the top. The wire is tied to the left bottom screw eye, fed through the screw eye on the left side of the recess, across to the screw eye on the right side of the recess, and down to the bottom right screw eye where it is secured. This type of wiring effectively distributes the stresses on the frame.

Metal sectional frames typically include the necessary hanging hardware. It takes the form of snap-in or screw-in hangers. Both work by being squeezed against the inside of the frame extrusion and are straightforward and easy to install. For large metal frames where the contents are heavy and the bottom of the frame threatens to sag or bow, the bottom of the frame can be reinforced by the installation of two extra hangers. Run a tension wire between them in the same manner described for the wood frame above and the bottom of the frame will be stabilized. Your final task in picture framing is simply attaching self-adhesive bumper pads to the back of the frame to protect the wall during hanging. Just peel off the release paper and place them on each corner.

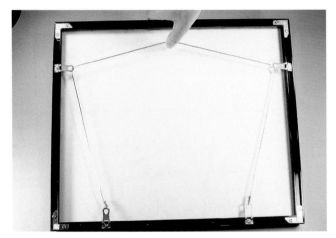

With heavier framed art where the bottom of the frame may sag or bow, the bottom of the frame can be reinforced by the installation of extra hangers.

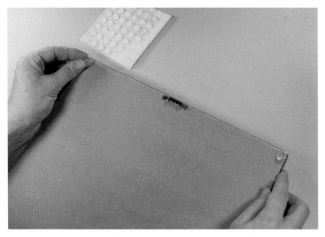

To attach self-adhesive bumpers, just peel off the release paper and place one on each corner.

The favored hanging device of most picture framers is the wall hook. Attached to the wall with a nail driven at an angle through a bend at the top of the hanger, this device is available in a selection of sizes and strengths to handle a variety of framed artwork. But when it comes to the question of strength, the hanger is only half the issue. How strong is the wall?

PLASTER WALLS present a problem in terms of cracking. One trick is to soften the plaster by making a small hole in the wall with an awl and injecting some water into the plaster. Another trick is to stick a piece of masking tape over the wall before hammering the nail in.

WALLBOARD may be too weak to support heavier art and an anchor bolt may have to be used in place of the hook. DRYWALL PICTURE HANGERS are one alternative. Incorporating a durable two-prong design, they can be hammered in within seconds and hold up to 60 pounds.

BRICK or CONCRETE WALLS are at the opposite end of the spectrum from wallboard, as they are too hard or dense to accept a nail. Your may have to drill into them, then insert a plastic sleeve to accept a screw.

A less labor-intensive approach is to use HARD-WALL PICTURE HANGERS, which are plastic hangers equipped with specially hardened steel pins that can be hammered into cement, cinder block, concrete, and soft brick.

For brick walls with at least ⅛" mortar joints between the bricks, BRICK CLIPS can be used. They snap on easily and support up to 25 pounds.

PICTURE HEIGHT ON THE WALL

Generally speaking, framed art should not be hung above eye level unless the ceiling is high. This may explain why it was fashionable in the nineteenth century to hang pictures high, at a time when ceilings were higher.

With modern lower ceilings, the general rule is to hang pictures so the eye of the viewer is at about the same level as the lower third of the picture. Naturally, the picture may have to be raised or lowered to accommodate furniture or offset it.

Like many areas of picture framing, formulas and rules can only take us so far. At some point, we run flat up against realities and have to be flexible. The same is true of any effort to frame for yourself efficiently and inexpensively.

You need to plan ahead and know what to expect, such as the type of wood your frame is made of (hard or soft?), the depth of the recess that will accept your sandwich, and the nature of the wall you plan to hang your work on, and then be willing to make the necessary adjustments in materials and techniques accordingly.

Moreover, you need to know just how far you are willing to go to emulate professionalism, and be prepared to invest a little extra to achieve that result. If you are willing to be flexible, you will achieve a satisfying result as you move through the last stages of your picture-framing project.

This familiar wall hook, which comes in many sizes and stengths, is attached to the wall with a nail driven at an angle through a bend in the top of the hanger.

AFTERWORD

It has been the objective of this book to take you step by step through the procedures involved in picture framing in a way that will let you understand and implement what you have learned. From the outset, this book was intended to be used, not just read once and shelved, and although these pages may have succeeded in opening your eyes to what matting, mounting, and framing are all about, they will have failed somewhat if they do not find their way into your hands as a reference in the future.

This book was actually designed with two objectives in mind: to take beginner home framers through the full process in a way that would make it understandable; and at the same time, to clarify for practicing framers some of the more esoteric techniques, shedding light on the more troubling mysteries and obstacles they've encountered.

The curious thing is, as the book fulfills its mission, it will transform its objectives, even while it remains in the hands of a single reader, because, for many, it will act first to make of them practicing framers, and then, later, to help them overcome obstacles and undertake new challenges. If it can do both of these things, this book will truly have accomplished its mission.

RESOURCES

American Frame Corp.
400 Tomahawk Drive
Maumee, OH 43537-1695
888-628-3833
800-893-3898 (fax)
www.americanframe.com
Offers a broad range of frames, matboard, and related items. Color catalog free; on-line catalog. Order by phone, fax, or on-line.

AMS — Art Materials Service, Inc.
625 Joyce Kilmer Avenue
New Brunswick, NJ 08901
888-522-5526
732-545-8888 (fax)
Manufacturer of hardware for picture framing. Contact for retailer list.

Artist and Display Supply
9015 West Burleigh Street
Milwaukee, WI 53222
414-442-9100
Retail store offering framing supplies and hands-on workshops on matting, mounting, and framing.

Black & Decker
626 Hanover Pike
Hampstead, MD 21074
800-544-6986
www.blackanddecker.com
Manufacturer of quality hand tools, saws, and workbenches. Contact for retailer list.

Daniel Smith
4150 First Avenue South
Seattle, WA 98134
Contact for other locations
800-426-6740
800-238-4065 (fax)
www.danielsmith.com
Supplier of art materials, including frames, matboard, and related items. Color catalog free; on-line catalog. Order by phone, fax, on-line, or in store.

Dick Blick
P. O. Box 1267
Galesburg, IL 61402-1267
Contact for other locations
800-828-4548
800-621-8293 (fax)
www.dickblick.com
Supplier of art materials, including frames, matboard, and related items. Color catalog free; on-line catalog. Order by phone, fax, on-line, or in store.

Fletcher-Terry Company
65 Spring Lane
Farmington, CT 06032
800-843-3826
860-676-8858 (fax)
www.fletcherterry.com
Manufacturer of point drivers, point inserting tools, and mat cutters. Contact for retailer list.

Frame Fit Company
Dept. ANE, P. O. Box 12727
Philadelphia, PA 19134
800-523-3693
800-344-7010 (fax)
www.framefit.com
Supplier of wood and metal picture frames. Order by phone or fax.

Frames by Mail
11440 Shenck Drive
St. Louis, MO 63043
800-332-2467
800-891-8801 (fax)
www.framesbymail.com
Supplier of wood and metal picture frames. Order by phone or fax.

Frame Tek, Inc.
512-D Market Square
Eugene, OR 97402
800-227-9934
541-431-4366 (fax)
www.frametek.com
Manufacturer of framing spacers. Contact for retailer list.

Framing4Yourself.com
271 East Helen Road
Palatine, IL 60067
800-246-4726
847-934-1474 (fax)
www.framing4yourself.com
Supplier of a wide range of frames, matboard, and related items. Hands-on framing workshops in many cities. On-line catalog. Order by phone, fax, or on-line.

Graphik Dimensions
2103 Brentwood Street
High Point, NC 27263
800-221-0262
336-887-3773 (fax)
www.pictureframes.com
Supplier of a wide range of frames, matboard, and related items. Color catalog free; on-line catalog. Order by phone, fax, or on-line.

International Paper
400 Atlantic Street
Stamford, CT 06921
800-223-1268
www.internationalpaper.com
Manufacturer of Queen City matboard and FomeCor® foamboard. Contact for retailer list.

Jerry's Art-a-Rama
5325 Departure Drive
Raleigh, NC 27616
Contact for other locations
800-827-8478
919-873-9565 (fax)
www.jerryscatalog.com
Supplier of art materials, including frames, matboard, and related items. Hands-on framing workshops. Color catalog free; on-line catalog. Order by phone, fax, on-line, or in store.

Light Impressions
P. O. Box 22708
Rochester, NY 14692-2708
800-828-6216
800-828-5539 (fax)
www.lightimpressionsdirect.com
Supplier of photography items, including frames and matboard. Color catalog free; on-line catalog. Order by phone, fax, or on-line.

Lineco
P. O. Box 2604
Holyoke, MA 01041
800-322-7775
800-298-7815 (fax)
www.lineco.com
Manufacturer of archival-quality mounting tapes and adhesives. Contact for retailer list.

Logan Graphic Products, Inc.
1100 Brown Street
Wauconda, IL 60084
800-331-6232
847-526-5155 (fax)
www.artproducts.com/logan
Manufacturer of mat cutters and related equipment. Contact for retailer list.

McIntosh Art Supply
2501 Montana Avenue
Billings, MT 59101
406-252-2010
Retail store offering framing supplies and hands-on workshops on matting, mounting, and framing.

Miller's Art Supply
279 West 9 Mile Road
Ferndale, MI 48220
248-414-7070
Retail store offering framing supplies and hands-on workshops on matting, mounting, and framing.

Moore Push-Pin Company
1300 East Mermaid Lane
Wyndmoor, PA 19038
215-233-5700
215-233-0660 (fax)
www.push.pin.com
Manufacturer of quality framing tapes and adhesives. Contact for retailer list.

Nielsen & Bainbridge, LLC
40 Eisenhower Drive
Paramus, NJ 07653
800-526-9073
800-656-6853 (fax)
www.nbframing.com
Manufacturer of Bainbridge Matboard, Nielsen Frames, and a wide range of related items. Contact for retailer list.

Pearl Paint
308 Canal Street
New York, NY 10013
Contact for other locations
800-221-6845
www.pearlpaint.com
Supplier of art materials, including frames, matboard, and related items. Hands-on framing workshops. Color catalog free. Order by phone, fax, on-line, or in store.

Seal® Brands from Hunt Corporation
2005 Market Street
Philadelphia, PA 19103
800-955-4868
www.sealbrands.com
Manufacturer of dry mounting, wet mounting, and laminating equipment and related framing items; Hunt also manufactures X-Acto knives and Boston paper trimmers. Contact for retailer list.

Stanley Tools
1000 Stanley Drive
New Britain, CT 06053
860-255-5111
860-827-3895 (fax)
www.stanleyworks.com
Manufacturer of quality hand tools. Contact for retailer list.

3M Stationery & Office Supplies Division
3M Center,
Building 223-38-03
St. Paul, MN 55144-1000
612-575-0928
612-736-8261 (fax)
www.mmm.com
Manufacturer of quality mounting tapes, adhesives, and dispensers. Contact for retailer list.

True-Vue, Inc.
1315 North Branch Street
Chicago, IL 60622-2413
800-282-8788
312-943-2938
www.true-vue.com
Manufacturer of glass, including nonglare and UV-protective. Contact for retailer list.

INDEX

Academic framing, 31, 32
Accents, 36–37, 112–113
Acid burn, 40, 116
Acid-free materials, 116
Acid-neutralized materials, 116
Acrylic, 44–45
  cutting of, 74
Adhesive hangers, 152
Adhesives, 51–52, 54, 56, 120, 121, 122
Adhesive transfer tape, 56, 64
Aerosol-spray adhesives, 51, 52, 120
Aesthetics, 21, 28
American Frame Corporation, 36, 47
Angle plate, 105
Archival framing, 39, 115, 116, 119
Artist, honoring color values of, 32, 33
Artwork sandwich, 144, 145, 146–147, 148
Assembling frames, 135–139

Backing sheet, 84–85
Bainbridge Artcare, 4, 12, 30, 38, 68, 82, 114, 134, 140
Balanced borders, 24, 26, 27, 28
Base cap molding, 75
Base shoe molding, 75
Beaded molding, 79
Bench-top router table, 66
Bevel cutting head, 59
Beveled molding, 79
Black & Decker, 62
Blade
  80-tooth carbide, 47, 65–66
  changing of, 85
Bleeds, 18, 19
Block-edged straightedge, 63
Board, mounting, 57
Bone folder, 87
Border finder, 21
Borders, 21–29
  bracketing, 92–94
Bottom line, 67
Box framing, 57, 81, 150
Box molding, 76
Bracketing borders, 92–94
Brackets
  corner, 55
  mounting fixtures as, 57, 58
Brad pusher, 63
Brads, 55, 63, 146
Brick clips, 155
Brick walls, 155

Buffered materials, 116
Bumper pads, self-adhesive, 47, 153
Burnishing bone, 87

Canvas, 14
  stretched, in frame, 149
Carbide blade, 80-tooth, 47, 65–66
Carrier paper, 19, 20
Chopped and routed frames, 46–47, 137
Chop service, 26
Clamps, corner, 47, 66
Cleaner, glass, 57
Clips
  brick, 155
  off-set, 55, 56, 148
  sawtooth, 47, 152
  spring, 47, 145
Cold mounting, 51, 52, 121
Color(s), 31–37
  choosing of, 34
  core, 42
  double mat, 34
  psychological response to, 37
Color balance, 32–35
Color specifier, 36
Color temperature, 33
Color values, of artist, 32, 33
Combination bevel cutting head and straight edge, 59
Commercial spacers, 15, 16, 58, 143
Concrete walls, 155
Condensation, moisture, 14, 40
Conservation framing, 39, 115, 116, 119
Construction moldings, 75
Cool colors, 33
Core colors, 42
Corner brackets, 55
Corner clamps, 47, 66
Corners
  matboard, 36, 37
  mounting, 54
Cotton-core matboard, 40, 41, 42
Coved molding, 75, 78
Covers, dust, 58, 62
Crescent, 51
Cross-stitch, 57
Cutter(s)
  glass, 64, 74
  mat, 59–62, 64, 72
Cutting
  of acrylic, 74
  of glass, 74

of length molding, 138
of mat windows, 83–113
Decorative accents, 36–37, 112–113
Double mat, 90–91
  color combinations in, 34, 36
Double multiple-opening mat, 95–97
Dry-mount press, 51, 52, 120
Dust covers, 58, 62, 150–151

Economizing, 10, 28, 67, 72, 151
Efficiency, 21, 28
Eight-sided window, 105–106
80-tooth carbide blade, 47, 65–66
Elevation mounting, 128
Equipment, 39, 59–67
Extension arm, 65

Face
  frame, 50
  mat, 112–113
Finishing molding, 80
Fitting art to frame, 15, 16
Fixtures, mounting, 57, 58
Flat molding, 77
Fletcher, 63
Floats, 19, 20
Foamboard, 42
40½" mat cutters, 60
Frame(s), 46–50
  assembling of, 135–139
  chopped and routed, 46–47, 137
  colors of, 36–37
  fitting art to, 15, 16
  irregular size, 22
  making of, 65–66, 75–79
  metal. See< Metal frame(s)
  over object box, 150
  standard. See Standard frame(s)
  stretched canvas in, 149
  wood. See Wood frame(s)
Frame fitting, 145–151
Framer, honoring of, 33
Framer's tool, 147
Frame shops, 23, 26, 36, 45, 46, 48, 52
Framing
  academic, 31, 32
  box, 57, 81, 150
  conservation, 39, 115, 116, 119
  museum, 40, 41, 42, 116, 117
  safe, regular, 118
French mat, 112–113

Glass, 14, 15, 16, 40, 44, 45, 58, 141
  cutting of, 74

Glass cleaner, 57
Glass cutter, 64, 74
Glazer's point, 147
Glazing, 44–45, 141, 142–143
Glue, wood, 57
Gummed linen tape, 53
Gummed paper tape, 53

Hammer, 62
Handheld mat cutters, 59, 60, 61
Hand tools, 62
Hangers, 55, 56, 152, 153, 154, 155
Hanging, of artwork, 154–155
Hanging hardware, 55–56, 152–153
Hanging wire, 47, 55, 152
Hardwall picture hangers, 155
Hardware, 55–56, 152–153
  with mail-order frame, 47
Height, picture, on wall, 155
Hinge-mounting tapes, 53, 123, 124, 125
Hinges, strap, 47
Honoring
  of artist's color values, 32, 33
  of framer, 33
Hunt Corporation, 52, 120

Indicator lines, cutter, 86–87
Industrial plunge router, 66
Inks, touch-up, 47
Installing
  of artwork sandwich, 144, 145–151
  of frame over object box, 150–151
  of stretched canvas, 149
Internet, 28, 36, 46–47, 48, 55, 57, 62
Irregular frame size, 22

J molding, 78
Joined frames, 46
Joining, of length molding, 138–139
Juried exhibitions, 31

Knives, 62, 72, 150
Kraft paper, 58, 150, 151

Length(s)
  lumber, 75
  molding in, 47–48, 138–139
  window, 18
Lignin-free materials, 116
Lineco, 53, 54
Linen tape, gummed, 53
Lites, 44, 45
Logan, 60, 61, 62, 65, 107, 109, 110–111
Looking good, 21, 28

Lumber lengths, 75

Mail order, 28, 36, 46–47, 48
Making frames, 65–66, 75–79
Marking, of mat, 88, 89
Mat
  double, 34, 90–91
  float, 19, 20
  marking of, 88, 89
  multiple-opening, 92–94, 95–97
  oval, 107–109
  round, 107–109
  single, 88–89
  stepped-corner, 103–104
  title indent, 98–99
  title window, 100–102
  V-groove, 110–111
Matboard, 40–42
  sizing of, 70–73
Mat cutters, 59–62, 64, 72
Materials, 39, 40–58
  preparing of, 69–81
Mat guide, setting of, 88
Mat knife, 62
Matted floats, 19, 20
Matting
  measuring for, 16–17
  pros and cons of, 14, 15
Mat window(s)
  cutting of, 83–113
  edges and dimensions of, 18
  eight-sided, 105–106
  oval/round, 109
  size of, 92
  title, 100–102
Measurements, 13–29
Measuring, for matting, 16–17
Metal frame(s)
  artwork sandwich for, 145
  assembling of, 136
  colors of, 36
  selection of, 49
Mirror hangers, 55, 152
Miter saw, power, 47, 65
Miter vice, 47, 66
Moisture condensation, 14, 40
Molding
  beaded, 79
  beveled, 79
  box, 76
  construction, 75
  coved, 75, 78
  flat, 77
  J, 78
  in lengths, 47–48, 138–139
  sanding and finishing of, 80
Money, saving of, 14, 21, 28, 67, 72,

151
Mount, sink, 127
Mounting, 51–54, 115–133
  elevation, 128
  needlework, 57, 129–130
  nonadhesive, 126
  permanent, 51–52, 120–122
  removable, 123–127
  three-dimensional objects, 131–133
Mounting board, 57
Mounting corners, 54
Mounting fixtures, 57, 58
Mounting/hinging tissue, 53
Mounting strips, self-adhesive, 54
Multiple-opening mat, 92–94
  double, 95–97
Museum framing, 40, 41, 42, 116, 117
Mylar pockets, 54, 126

Nail set, 146
Needlenose pliers, 63
Needlework, 57, 129–130
Nielsen, 4, 12, 30, 38, 68, 82, 114, 134, 140
Nonadhesive mounting, 126
Noncontact adhesives, 54
Nonglare glass, 44

Object box, 57, 81, 131–133, 150
Objectives, 13
Odd-size art, into standard frame, 15, 16
Offset clips, 55, 56, 148
Offset corner mat, 103–104
Oval mat, 64, 107–109
Overcuts, 86
Overmat, 90

Paper, 14, 18–20
  carrier, 19, 20
  kraft, 58, 150, 151
  release, 121
Paper tape, gummed, 53
Pastel art, 128
Permanent mounting, 51–52, 120–122
pH balanced materials, 116
Phillips, 62
pH neutral materials, 116
Picture hangers, hardwall, 155
Picture height, on wall, 155
Picture wire, 47, 55, 152
Pins, straight, 57
Planning ahead, 14–17, 28
Plaster walls, 154
Plexiglas, 44–45

Pliers, 63
Plies, 84
Plunge router, 66
Point driver, 63, 147
Point pusher, 63, 147
Points, 147
Point squeezer, 63
Positionable Mounting Adhesive, 51–52, 122
Posters, 16
Power miter saw, 47, 65
Preassembled frames, 23, 28
Preparing materials, 69–81
Presses
  dry-mount, 51, 52, 120
  vacuum, 51, 52
Previewing color results, 36
Proportions, 13–29
Psychological response to color, 37
Purchase options, equipment, 67
Purpose, 13
PushMate, 63

Rabbet, frame, 48, 49, 50
Rack, frames off, 23, 28, 46
Reading ruler, 17
Regular framing, 118
Regular glass, 44
Regular matboard, 41, 42
Reinforced hinge mounts, 124, 125
Release paper, 121
Removable mounting, 123–127
Resources, 157–158
Retail-tax identification form, 46
Round mat, 64, 107–109
Routers, 66
Rulers, 17, 18
Rules to live by, 18–20

Safe, regular framing, 118
Sanding molding, 80
Saving money and time, 14, 21, 28, 67, 72, 151
Saw
  10" table, 66
  power miter, 47, 65
Sawtooth clips, 47, 152
Saw-toothed hangers, 55
Scotch, 52, 56, 64. See also 3M Corporation
Screwdrivers, 62
Screw eyes, 55, 56, 152
Screws, 47, 50, 56, 62
Seal, 51, 52, 120
Sectional frames, metal, 136

Securing contents, in wood frames, 63
Self-adhesive bumper pads, 153
Self-adhesive mounting strips, 54
Serrated corner brackets, 55
Shades, 32
Shank router, 2-horsepower, 66
S-hinge, reinforced, 124, 125
Side borders, narrower vs. wider, 66
Simple floats, 20
Single mat, 88–89
Sink mount, 127
Size(s)
  frame, irregular, 22
  mat window, 92
  standard, noncorrelation of, 24
Sizing
  glazing, 74
  matboard, 70–73
Slip sheet, 84–85
Spacers, 15, 16, 58, 143
Spray adhesives, 51, 52, 120
Spring clips, 47, 145
Squaring arm, 60
Standard frame(s)
  efficiency of, 23
  oddsize art into, 15, 16
  sizes of, 16, 23
Standard lites, 44, 45
Standard matboard sheet, 71
Standard sizes, noncorrelation of, 24
Starting borders, 21
Stepped-corner mat, 103–104
Straightedge, 18
  bevel cutting head and, 59
  and handheld cutter, 59, 61, 62, 63
Straight pins, 57
Strap hangers, 47, 55, 56, 152
Stretched canvas, in frame, 149

Table, bench-top router, 66
Table saw, 10," 66
Tape(s)
  hinge-mounting, 53, 123, 124, 125
  transfer, 56, 64
Tape measures, 18
Tax, use, 46
Temperature, color, 33
10" table saw, 66
T-hinge, reinforced, 124, 125
32" mat-cutting system, 59, 61, 72
Three-dimensional objects.
  See Object box
3M Corporation, 52, 56, 64, 112
Time, saving of, 21, 28

Tints, 32
Tissue, mounting/hinging, 53
Title indent mat, 98–99
Title window mat, 100–102
Tool(s)
  framer's, 147
  hand, 62
  for securing contents in wood frames, 63
Touch-up inks, 47
Transfer tape, 56, 64
2-horsepower 1/4" shank router, 66

Undercuts, 86
Underlayment, 84–85
Undermat, 90
"United Inches," 21
Use tax, 46
Usona Home Furnishings, 68
Utility knife, 62, 72
UV-protective glass, 44

Vacuum press, 51
Values, color, of artist, 32, 33
V-groove mat, 64, 110–111
V-hinge, reinforced, 124, 125
Vice, miter, 47, 66

Wallboard, 154–155
Wall Buddies, 55
Wall hook, 154
Walls, 154–155
Warm colors, 33
Weighted borders, 25, 26, 27, 28
White, 34, 35
Wholesalers, 23, 26, 46, 48
Width, window, 18
Window(s), mat. *See* Mat window(s)
Wire, hanging/picture, 47, 55, 152
Wood, type of, 50
Wood frame(s)
  artwork sandwich in, 146–147, 148
  assembling of, 137
  colors of, 36
  securing contents in, 63
  selection of, 48
Wood glue, 57
Workbench, 65

X-Acto knife, 150

Yardsticks, 18
Yellow pages, 46